Soul-Searching

Seeking Scientific Ground
for the Jewish Tradition
of an Afterlife

Yaakov Astor

TARGUM/FELDHEIM

First published 2003
Copyright © 2003 by Yaakov Astor
ISBN 1-56871-249-9

All rights reserved

No part of this publication may be translated, reproduced, stored in a retrieval system, or transmitted in any form or by any means, electronic, mechanical, photocopying, recording, or otherwise, without prior permission in writing from both the copyright holder and the publisher.

Published by:
Targum Press, Inc.
22700 W. Eleven Mile Rd.
Southfield, MI 48034
E-mail: targum@netvision.net.il
Fax: 888-298-9992
www.targum.com

Distributed by:
Feldheim Publishers
202 Airport Executive Park
Nanuet, NY 10954
www.feldheim.com

Printed in Israel

Marcheshvan 18, 5763

Rabbi Yaakov Astor, *shlita* — a distinguished *talmid chacham*, scholar and author, has written a fascinating book entitled, "Soul Searching," Seeking Scientific Ground for the Jewish Tradition of an Afterlife.

The book, in a most erudite, scholarly and yet readable fashion attempts quite successfully to do just that. This presentation can be extremely useful for both the serious theologian as well as the interested layman. I genuinely recommend this book as an important addition to one's library.

Sincerely,
Rabbi Mordechai Tendler

Contents

Preface 9
Foreword by Rabbi Ezriel Tauber 13
Introduction 21

LIFE AFTER LIFE

Thinking the Unthinkable 25
Soul Evidence 31
Journey of the Soul 45
The Out-of-Body Experience 51
The Laws of Mourning and the
   Out-of-Body Experience 57
The Tunnel 66
The Light 71
The Life Review 80

PAST LIVES

Reincarnation and Jewish Tradition 93
Many Lives 105
But Is It Science? 112
Past Lives, Past Debts, Living Lessons 137

LIFE

A Philosophy of Soul 157

APPENDIXES
   Appendix A: Afterlife in Scripture 175
   Appendix B: Hints of Soul 183

Bibliography. 189

Preface

In January of 1993, psychiatrist Dr. Brian Weiss spoke at a symposium in Florida on the subject of his best-selling book, *Many Lives, Many Masters*. At the same symposium, Rabbi Ezriel Tauber, a chassidic rabbi, was asked to speak as well. The evening was a success, and these two men, from two entirely different worlds, eventually agreed to produce a book together.

At the time, I was employed by Rabbi Tauber to transcribe his taped lectures and turn them into books. When Rabbi Tauber asked me to undertake the project on his and Dr. Weiss's behalf, my job was to produce a book centered around the intriguing dialogue between a "world-renowned psychiatrist and a hassidic rabbi."

The project met with numerous snags from the outset, not the least of which was that, living as they were at opposite ends of the East Coast, sitting the two together in the same room turned out to be more wishful thinking than reality. Indeed, only one such meeting ever took place. Since both men were extremely busy, literally flying all over the country and the world at a dizzying pace, even coordinating a phone call between them proved incredibly difficult. Nevertheless, combining my own research with individual exchanges with each man, I was eventually able to put together a book entitled *Soul-Searching: Explorations into the Science and Mystery of Immortality*.

Burdened with extremely busy schedules and now involved with writing other books of their own, Dr. Weiss and Rabbi Tauber, despite their initial enthusiasm, began to steer their energies elsewhere. *Soul-Searching* seemed dead.

Notwithstanding these setbacks, I maintained belief in the value of the book. I knew that here was an immensely fascinating topic with an unusual potential for mass appeal. That's when I got the idea that *Soul-Searching* needed to be resurrected, or at least reincarnated.

In truth, the present form is not vastly different from the original. Generally it places a greater emphasis on the Jewish texts and how they seem to have anticipated the findings of contemporary science. The original also had more quotes and opinions from Dr. Weiss and Rabbi Tauber. Overall, however, the effect is the same: a powerful and enjoyable reading experience with the potency to change the life of anyone who has done some serious soul-searching — anyone who has been seeking answers to life's most important questions.

On that note, let me take this opportunity to express

my sincere gratitude to both men. The power of the true story told in *Many Lives, Many Masters* is only as powerful as the man who wrote about it. If one's main question after reading *Many Lives* is "How do I know he did not make this up?" let me assure you that every encounter I and others have had with Dr. Weiss only strengthens the conviction that this is a man of integrity. His integrity is matched by his sincere concern for others, typically conveyed with exceptional warmth, patience, intelligence, and humility as well as a sense of humor. It has truly been a privilege to work with him.

For almost six years I wrote books for Rabbi Tauber. Besides the content, which is covered in eleven published volumes, I gained a depth and methodology for analyzing the teachings of our Sages and a way of viewing life that makes me indebted to him forever.

I once told myself that if I ever published a book I would not waste readers' time with acknowledgments. However, when one finally comes to the end of the excruciatingly long and arduous process of putting even as thin a volume as this out on the market, one is overwhelmed with the awareness of and gratitude for all those who made it possible.

My editor, Suri Brand, along with Miriam Zakon, Rabbi Dombey, and the staff of Targum Press impressed me from the start with their attention to detail, enthusiasm, and ability to give sound guidance.

Great thanks must be given to the many friends who

read earlier versions of the manuscript and without whose input and encouragement I could not have continued.

My parents, who gave me physical life, have given me much more than that. The idealism and honesty that have led me down the path I have traversed are their legacy. All I can claim, if I can claim anything, is to have merely followed through on qualities they possess.

To my children, you make it all worth it.

To my *eishes chayil*, a special soul filled and overflowing with unconditional love and encouragement, you are ultimately what has made this and everything in our lives possible.

Finally, all acknowledgments and gratitude ultimately go back to the Source, to the One who first breathed a living soul into us and then gave it this vast — no, endless — sea of wisdom called the Torah in which to swim and delight. "If Your Torah had not been my delight, I should have perished in my affliction" (Psalms 119:92).

Yaakov Astor
23 Shevat 5763

Foreword

by Rabbi Ezriel Tauber

> In the sixth hundredth year of Noah's life...all the fountains of the great depth were broken apart, and the windows of heaven were opened....
>
> *Genesis 7:11*

> In the six hundredth year of the sixth [millennium], the gates of wisdom above and the wellsprings of wisdom below will be opened, and the world will be uplifted to prepare for the ascension of the seventh [millennium], just as a person prepares himself toward sunset for the Sabbath.
>
> *Zohar I:117a*

The "sixth century of the sixth millennium" corresponds precisely with that outburst of scientific knowledge — the "wellsprings of wisdom below" — known as the Industrial Revolution. The contemporary world has been transformed by technology that those living before its advent could only have called "miraculous." And this explosion of knowledge continues today, only getting stronger with the passage of time, like the floodwaters of Noah piling up upon each other.

This outburst is not limited to the "lower waters," however. The explosion of "upper waters" today that began in the sixth millennium shapes so much of the Jewish world. The great spiritual revival movement led by the Ba'al Shem Tov and his disciples, as well as the yeshivah movement spearheaded by the Vilna Gaon and his disciples, are among the examples of powerful upper waters flowing into the world from the "sixth century of the sixth millennium."

Sometimes the upper and lower waters mingle, and this can describe perhaps the phenomenon of science attempting to address the issue of life after death. As this beautifully written, well-documented book — a veritable *Permission to Believe* on the afterlife — shows, scientific investigators have found a lot to say on the matter. And what they say, in consonance with what our tradition has always said, has powerful repercussions.

I was once witness to some of this power when I was invited to speak at a seminar in Montreal. A participant asked me how we could know there is a soul that survives bodily death. I answered citing some of the case studies of Dr. Ian Stevenson and others, which are detailed in this book.

After the lecture, one of the other lecturers, a French-born rabbi, Moshe Pell, told me that he became observant because of such an incident. He had been a student of psychology in a French university, taking part in a class on hypnosis where a young woman was being hypnotized. Suddenly, under trance, this French-speaking patient began speaking perfect English, recounting in detail the life of a woman who had lived a century before in England and who had died at childbirth, which she was reexperiencing in the hypnotic state. She was eventually guided out of the trance and back to her normal self. Her normal self, though, did not know a word of English. Yet she had just been speaking perfect English as she relived the fatal childbirth of this woman in a previous life!

Although I believed this possible, because the Torah says so, I asked the rabbi if he had a tape of the session. To my surprise, he said yes and eventually got me a copy. Everything was just as he said.

The experience was so powerful it compelled this French psychology student to examine his Jewish roots, conclude it was true, and even become a rabbi who teaches Torah to others.

We have to ask why this explosion of information is happening in our days. Why did the *Zohar* long ago predict this torrential downpour of wisdom at this time? The answer must be that this knowledge is paving the way for the Messianic Era, when the "knowledge of God will cover the earth like the waters cover the seas" (Isaiah 11:9). This knowledge, however, does not come without costs. The more one is exposed to such knowledge, the more one has to take it out of the realm of theory and into practice.

"Our task is to learn, to become God-like through knowledge," Dr. Brian Weiss's remarkable patient, Catherine, tells him in his immensely popular *Many Lives, Many Masters*. "By knowledge we approach God...." This is eerily similar to the way Maimonides put it almost one thousand years ago:

> One can love God only as much as the knowledge with which he knows Him. A small amount [of knowledge] arouses a lesser love. A greater amount, a greater love.
>
> *Mishnah Torah, Hilchot Teshuvah 10:6*

The purpose here is not to prove Jewish tradition. Scientifically trained people are beginning to see things the way we have always seen them. We believe in our tradition because it proves itself in so many ways all the time and ultimately because we are "believers, the descendants of believers" who stood at Sinai. Nevertheless, this intermingling of the wisdom of the "lower waters" and the "upper waters" adds strength to our belief as much as it causes others to rethink theirs.

We should not be surprised, though, that not every person who is presented with these ideas changes his whole life overnight. "Truth sprouts from the earth" (Psalms 85:15). Truth is like a seed. It doesn't necessarily sprout the moment you place it in the ground. It needs time and water — that is, wisdom. Generally speaking, any long-lasting change is change that comes about gradually, through a realistic process of gaining knowledge day by day. Intellectual knowledge must become emotionalized through everyday practice and action. Then the knowledge becomes real and permanent.

This book can serve as an important part of that process, both to the person long committed to observance and to the one first inquiring into it. It is not a magic potion, however. Some people read or even experience the things described in this book but do not change. Or they change a little, but do not follow through with what they've learned all the way. The greater the knowledge, the greater the responsibility to do something with the knowledge. The more one waters one's outlook with the waters of true knowledge, the more life will sprout.

My hope is that this book will become a serious tool that brings forth life for those who desire life.

*We are but of yesterday
and know nothing,
for our days upon earth
are but a shadow.*

Job 8:9

Our days are a fleeting shadow.

Psalms 144:4

Introduction

This book was born from a passionate yearning to know the deepest mysteries of existence. And what is deeper than the mystery of death — which is but a doorway to the greater mystery of life?

At the same time, this passion created a contradiction. Years of research and reflection have led to many discoveries and profound insights. Yet the pursuit of clarification can allow a person to delude himself that he understands the mystery.

I admit I do not understand the mystery.

I do not understand the mystery of the afterlife.

I do not understand the mystery of life itself.

Yet if I have not in any way dented the mystery of existence, I have accomplished at least one thing: I have discovered that I am a soul-searcher. This book does not claim to rob anyone of the privilege of claiming that life beyond this life is anything but the most profound of mysteries. All this book does is share insights from which fellow soul-searchers along the path in this odyssey called life can perhaps gain.

For those with significant exposure to the authentic Jewish sources, this book brings together numerous original sources on topics such as the soul and afterlife. For those with little background, this book should be an eye-opener because there is often a remarkable congruency between images of an afterlife in modern, scientific accounts and traditional Jewish sources. Over and over again the two seem to be discussing a similar reality.

Long ago the Sages called this life a corridor for life in the next world (*Avot* 4:16). The reverse is also true: contemplation about life in the next world leads us to an appreciation of life in this world and our place in it. Awareness of our mortality helps us view this life in a more vibrant and meaningful way. And so the ultimate goal of this book is to help others experience life — this life — more fully, vibrantly, and passionately.

LIFE AFTER LIFE

Thinking the Unthinkable

> For most Westerners, life after death has become unthinkable and — along with death itself — a tabooed subject.... Most thinking Westerners would rather not think about: What will happen to me after I die?
>
> Dr. Ian Stevenson, *Children Who Remember Past Lives*[1]

Sooner or later each of us is confronted with the question of our own mortality. And, for better or worse, the awareness of our mortality compels us to address the core, to reflect upon our true identities, to seek answers to that ultimate question of questions: Who am I?

And yet, because mortality is a key unlocking the doorway to our selves, we rarely use it. We're so afraid that we will open the door and find nothing there that we keep the key far out of sight to prevent it from reminding us that there is a door to be unlocked. Is it any wonder that we design our lives so that we will be busy from dawn to dusk with activities that rob us of the time to take up the meaning of life soberly?

No matter what we do, though, the question will not go away. Life will always remind us — sometimes gently, sometimes more forcibly — about the possibility of death.

Most of us want to believe that life has meaning and that true happiness is our manifest destiny. Existential angst and lament lead nowhere. How, though, does an educated person today come to an experiential, genuine conviction that there is a deeper meaning beneath the surface of his or her life? That this life is not an end-all? That there is a greater destiny waiting? That consciousness persists beyond the grave — indeed, that each of us is a deposit of immortality?

That is the question. And it is a question with enormous ramifications for our well-being *in this life*. An often heard remark, especially from those in grief or people afflicted with terminal illness, is "I would like to believe it [the existence of an afterlife], and it would give me great comfort, but I just can't. I don't know how to believe."

And so it is with many educated people today. Whether it is fear of the potential pain associated with death, the fear of terminating relationships with loved ones, the fear of the unknown, the fear of being alone, the fear over the prospect of nonexistence, or some other related fear, the inability to satisfactorily address life's one certainty — death —

creates an existential emptiness one need not even be cognizant of to feel its effects.

Carl Jung said he had never met a patient over thirty-five whose problems did not root back to fear of his approaching death.[2] Author Dr. Larry Dossey says that "fear of death has caused more misery in human history than all the diseases put together."[3] Perhaps no one has more poignantly or poetically summed up the situation than King David, who likened this life to a "valley overshadowed by death."[4] Indeed, the fear of death is an ever-present subconscious, if not conscious, anxiety hanging over and all around us, producing its own kind of psychological fallout that can permeate life until it slowly eats away at a person's well-being.

One way or another, each of us lives with the anxiety of death. Sadly, few deal with that fact until they hit forty-something or until a desperate situation is forced upon them. It is sad because, despite whatever negative fallout fear of death can inflict upon the psyche, it can sensitize a person to a beautiful side of life as nothing else.

We take life for granted. The fish, whose whole being is in the sea, does not feel the water. Only when it raises its head above the surface does it become aware of the absence of the water that sustains it. A human being, whose being is in "life," does not feel "life" until it is almost taken away. Our vision is clouded by a myopia called life. In order to understand life we must somehow get outside of it.

One way of getting outside it is to go through what is

commonly called a near-death experience. As one such person put it,

> I remember I knew that everything everywhere in the universe was okay, that the plan was perfect. That whatever was happening — the wars, famine, whatever — was okay. Everything was perfect.... And the whole time I was in that state...I was just an infinite being...knowing that...you're home forever. That you're safe forever. And that everybody else was.[5]

Research has shown that survivors of near death (what is called "a near-death experience," or "NDE" for short) are almost all changed for the good. They grow up to be physically healthier and have fewer psychosomatic complaints. They are happier, exhibit stronger family ties, show more zest for living, and have a greatly diminished fear of death. Similarly, they tend to do more community work, give more charity, and often work in professions that involve helping people.[6] Even those who had a near-death experience as the result of a suicide attempt were found to be significantly less likely to try it again.[7]

Not surprisingly, studies also confirm that virtually everyone who has had an actual NDE invariably comes to some kind of belief in an afterlife, even those who formerly considered themselves atheists.[8] It follows, then, that the discovery and awareness of one's immortality is the foundation of a healthy psychological constitution. At the very least, it can be said that conviction in one's immortality radically improves the quality of one's present life.

Short of nearly dying, though, is there a way to turn fear of death into zest for life?

Yes. That is one of the underlying assumptions of this book. The secret is having a vista open up, a new perspective that transcends our inherent myopia. One who comes to genuinely view this existence in a larger perspective weathers life's frustrations more easily and revels in its triumphs more intensely than those who do not attain that same high ground. On the other hand, one who cannot see through the mirror of temporary, physical existence feels truly bereft of life, true life. Time in such a sense is experienced as nothing more than destruction of the moment. Such people have no choice other than to seek to kill time. Their days are truly a fleeting shadow.

Consequently, one of the most important conclusions anyone can draw while submerged in life's myopia — in this fishbowl of existence overshadowed by death — is that he possesses an immortal soul. How to help the educated, contemporary person feel more at ease with that is the first issue we need to address.

Notes

1. *Children Who Remember Past Lives* (University Press of Virginia, 1987), p. 317. Dr. Stevenson is the foremost researcher into life and death issues. He graduated with an M.D. from

McGill University at Montreal in 1943 at the top of his class. In 1957, at the age of thirty-nine, he became head of the department of psychiatry at the University of Virginia School of Medicine. It was there that he began his research into reports of children who remembered past lives. Eventually he gave up his administrative duties to become a full-time researcher of paranormal phenomena. His work — consisting of some two thousand cases — is characterized by its meticulous documentation and cross-checking (see also part 2, the chapter entitled, "But Is It Science?").

2. Jung writes: "During the past thirty years people from all civilized countries of the earth have consulted me. I have treated many hundreds of patients, the largest number being Protestants, the smaller number Jews, and [about] five or six believing Catholics. Among all my patients in the second half of my life — that is to say, over thirty-five — there has not been one whose problem in the last resort was not that of finding a religious outlook on life. It is safe to say that every one of them fell ill because he had lost that which the living religions of every age have given to their followers, and none of them has been really healed who did not regain his religious outlook" (*Modern Man in Search of a Soul*, p. 244).

3. *Reinventing Medicine*, p. 25.

4. Psalms 23:4.

5. *Heading Toward Omega*, by Kenneth Ring, p. 62.

6. Melvin Morse, M.D., and Paul Perry have an entire book on the subject: *Transformed by the Light: The Powerful Effects of Near-Death Experiences on People's Lives*.

7. Melvin Morse and Paul Perry, *Transformed by the Light*.

8. Kenneth Ring, *Heading Toward Omega*, p. 85.

Soul Evidence

> Any persons who are not sufficiently persuaded of the existence...of the soul...I wish them to know that all other things of which they perhaps think themselves more assured (such as possessing a body and that there are stars and an earth and so on) are less certain.
>
> *Descartes*

The Bible says, "God blew into his [man's] nostrils the eternal soul [literally, the soul or breath of life]."[1] One of the foremost commentators of the Bible, Nachmanides, comments on that verse, "The One who blows, blows from within Himself." The symbolism implies that there is a real divine spark within us. By its very essence, the human soul is immortal. It has to live on, somehow, after death.

Since the nineteenth century the Bible has lost prestige

in the eyes of many an educated Westerner. Yet is an idea like soul really heretical to or outside the framework of twentieth-century discoveries or philosophies? Upon close inspection, it clearly is not. Consider, for instance, the contemporary viewpoint on the two most basic elements of all life: time and space.

Everything we comprehend must exist within time and space. Yet what do time and space consist of? At the beginning of the modern age, scientists discovered that the basic substance of physical space was the atom. Then they found that the atom itself was made of smaller particles (such as protons and neutrons). Then they realized that the smaller particles, too, must be made of even smaller particles (quarks, neutrinos). Then physicists came to speak simply of waves of energy, and then particle-wave duality (Louis de Broglie, 1924), and now, even more mysteriously, dark matter.[2] Where does it end? Does it end? What is the substance of the physical world?

If the essential substance of physical space is a mystery, then time is even more unfathomable. "Life in our world," a great thinker once wrote, "has no present.... It has no permanence. This life is influenced by time, which has no duration. No time, whether it be a second or an instant or even a fraction or even a part thereof, is comprehensible. It is merely a combination of past and future. No sooner does one utter the word *instant* or even begin to pronounce its first syllable than the future has slipped by and become the past. Our very existence is a swift flight in pursuit of the future, which, as soon as it appears, becomes transformed into the past."[3]

Like space, time has no substance. Yet if everything we understand and experience must occur within time and space, what then is the substance of our lives? Indeed, the words of the psalmist are literally true: our "days are but a fleeting shadow."[4]

For well over a century, science, empiricism, rationalism, and the like have dominated society's outlook. Among other things, this century of skepticism has succeeded in creating an intellectual establishment increasingly close-minded to the possibility of a life beyond the grave. It's been said that the topic of an afterlife has been one of the taboos of the modern, scientific age. Be that as it may, cracks in this wall of denial always existed and even started becoming more pronounced in the latter half of this century.

In 1975, Raymond Moody Jr., MD, Ph.D., wrote a phenomenally popular and influential book entitled *Life After Life*. In it he relayed numerous cases of people who had "died" and been resuscitated. Many had been clinically dead for as long as two minutes, five minutes, even ten minutes and more. Surprisingly, these people did not experience a black nothingness, but rather a very rich, vivid procession of sensations involving many senses. From a strict medical standpoint, they should have seen or felt nothing. Yet, not only could they see and feel, but they experienced sensations that were larger than life, including floating above their bodies and watching the impassioned efforts of others to revive them, traveling through a type of tunnel, and encountering deceased relatives or beings of light, or experiencing an all-encompassing warm, restorative light.

Studying the cases, Dr. Moody isolated several recurring themes. Although no two NDEs were identical, at the core were a slew of common experiences. The fact that so many different people who did not know each other related very similar experiences suggested that the phenomenon was authentic. His work, along with the more scientifically rigorous work of subsequent others, showed that there was an unchanging core near-death experience that remained more or less constant across gender, race, culture, and even history.[5]

Life After Life was a breakthrough. Millions of people read it. Its success launched a new field of scientific endeavor: the near-death experience. Teams of researchers around the globe took up serious study of the phenomenon. And the evidence continues to mount.

Perhaps the most impressive research conducted post–*Life After Life* involves cases with children. Most children, in their innocence, do not have the motivations to create a hoax, and those who might stretch the truth probably do not know enough about the details of the phenomenon to get away with it. Thus the younger the child when he or she nearly died, the more impressive the account.

Study of NDEs of children has been the pet project of clinician-researcher Dr. Melvin Morse, who, in addition to contributing to medical journals, has authored two well-received books on the subject. In his *Closer to the Light*,[6] he reports the impressive case of Mark, who nearly died when he was only nine months old. Of course, a nine-month-old cannot verbalize his experience. But when Mark turned three, his parents brought him to a holiday pageant where a play had been enacted. "That [person in the play] was not [God]," he innocently told his parents afterward.

Mark went on to explain that he knew this because he had run "through fields with God" after he had floated above his body in the emergency room two years before! His startled parents listened to him tell how he "flew out of the room" into the waiting room, where he had seen his grandmother and grandfather crying, thinking he was going to die. He told his parents that he had crawled up a tunnel, and at the end was a bright place, which contained the field where he "ran with God."

Mark's description of the doctors and nurses working on him in the emergency room and his grandparents waiting outside crying was accurate. This is especially impressive because his parents never told him that he had nearly died when he was nine months old. Spontaneously, at the age of three, Mark somehow knew he had almost died once. He somehow knew he had been in an emergency room and that his grandparents were crying in the waiting room next door. He somehow knew many of the typical core experiences of the NDE, yet at the age of three he had never been exposed to those details.

In another case reported by Dr. Morse, an eleven-year-old boy had cardiac arrest in the lobby of a hospital. He heard a buzzing sound in his ears and was "whooshed" out of his body (one of the common NDE experiences). He then floated above the site and observed, in a very detached manner, efforts to revive him. He saw doctors place paddles on his body to revive his heart and yell, "Stand back!" and "Press the button!" When they did so, suddenly he was no longer on the ceiling looking down, but back in his body looking up at the doctors and nurses. Surprised, he said, "That was weird. I was floating above my body and was sucked back into myself."

Nurses at the scene corroborated that he made that statement right at the moment of resuscitation. They also confirmed the sequence of events as the boy described. Why would an eleven-year-old say, "That was weird. I was floating above my body and was sucked back into myself," at the moment he was resuscitated if not for the fact that his mind was present and observing from above the entire time? Only if the experience of getting "sucked" back into his body was so "weird" that he had to relate it immediately — only then do his words begin to make sense. How else could he have the presence of mind to say this in that situation?

These are only two examples of many, many such cases. There is now a plethora of books on the subject of near-death experiences available to the public. Be that as it may, such studies comprise only one component of the investigation into the possibility of life after life and only the most popular and recent kind at that.

Serious scientific attempts into substantiating the existence of survival beyond bodily death actually began over a century ago. In the last quarter of the nineteenth century, a "remarkable group of distinguished scientists and scholars" took an active interest in applying the scientific method to the study of various phenomena deemed paranormal. Henri Bergson and William James are just two of the more prominent names included in the group that formed or supported the Society for Psychical Research. James himself wrote, "Were I asked to point to a scientific journal where hard-headedness and never-sleeping suspicion of sources of error might be seen in their full bloom, I think I should have to fall back on the *Proceedings of the Society for Psychical Research*."[7]

For over a century now such researchers have conducted studies, and though not all of it is widely accepted, an undeniable breakthrough has occurred in at least one area: the authenticity of extrasensory perception, or ESP. The existence of extrasensory perception demonstrates that we have abilities that are impossible to explain by purely materialistic, mechanistic explanations. If nothing else, it shows that we must be more than our physical bodies.[8] And if we are more than our physical bodies, then we have a rational basis for the belief that something can survive bodily death.

Dr. H. J. Eysenck, renowned in the field of psychology, summed it up this way:

> Unless there is a gigantic conspiracy involving

some thirty university departments all over the world and several hundred highly respected scientists in various fields, many of them originally hostile to claims of the psychical researchers, the only conclusion the unbiased observer can come to must be that there does exist a small number of people who obtain knowledge existing in other people's minds or in the outer world by means as yet unknown to science."[9]

That very cautious assessment amounts to the unavoidable conclusion that extrasensory perception or telepathy exists. And if so, then, according to another renowned researcher, Dr. Ian Stevenson, a classic tenet of twentieth-century Western science and medicine is seriously challenged — namely, the almost dogmatic belief that "human personality consists of nothing but the expressions of the molecules and cells of which our physical bodies are built."[10] The bottom line is "The phenomena of telepathy...are not an alternative to survival after death, but a virtual guarantee of it."[11]

Evidence demonstrating the validity of some type of extra-bodily existence (and hence survival of some aspect of personality beyond death) also comes from research into the phenomenon called out-of-body experiences. The nine-month-old and eleven-year-old boys in Dr. Morse's files mentioned above are typical of such experiences.

Dr. Moody, too, records many such cases in his books, including, for instance, the report of a patient who, during a near-death experience, purportedly floated above her body and then outside the hospital walls where she saw a shoe sitting on a ledge of the multistory building. The shoe was later found to be at the exact spot on the ledge the patient described.

Other respected researchers, like Dr. Kenneth Ring,[12] also have in their files many out-of-body reports, such as the following:

> Bang! I left! The next thing I was aware of was floating on the ceiling.... From where I was looking, I could look down on this enormous fluorescent light...and it was so dirty on top of the light.... And I remember thinking, *Got to tell the nurses about that.*

To satisfy the scientific community's need for verification, Dr. Michael Sabom conducted experiments involving NDE patients who claimed to have out-of-body experiences. After hearing detailed accounts of the procedures performed on them, which they ostensibly witnessed from outside their bodies, he interviewed the medical team involved, talked to the family members, and checked the medical records to compare the details.

His findings were impressive. Not only did even medically ignorant NDE patients give significantly more accurate accounts of the efforts to save their lives than the control group (cardiac patients who did not have NDEs but were asked to describe their ordeals), but the NDE patients could do things like accurately describe the readings on machines not in their "line of sight even if their eyes had been open."[13]

Out-of-body experiences, then, add another dimension to the argument for the existence of a soul or afterlife.

Yet another avenue of research, surprisingly, comes from studies conducted to measure the effectiveness of prayer. Dr. Larry Dossey, a doctor who was previously skeptical to the idea, reviewed 131 experiments that he considered tight studies designed to examine whether some intentional mental act (such as prayer) could influence a living system.

What caught his attention initially was a San Francisco study conducted by a cardiologist on nearly four hundred patients, some of whom had been randomly prayed for. Characteristic of all well-done scientific studies, it was double-blind, meaning that the patients, doctors, and nurses did not know who was being prayed for and who was not.

The results were eye-opening. Individuals in the group who were prayed for were significantly better off (for instance, five times less likely to need antibiotics) than those who were not prayed for.

The San Francisco study interested Dr. Dossey enough to pursue the question on his own. Reviewing the 131 studies, which form the basis of his book *Healing Words*, he found impressive results in more than half of those studies. Over and over again people who were prayed for showed significantly greater improvement than those who were not prayed for. Improvements included lowered blood pressure and quicker healing of wounds. Even the effects of prayer on nonhuman life forms such as bacteria, fungi, seeds, and grains were shown to have a scientifically verifiable positive effect!

Dr. Dossey's conclusion was that "the evidence is simply overwhelming that prayer" works regardless of time or distance. Moreover, he infers that "these studies constitute empirical, indirect evidence for the existence of something we in the West have always called a 'soul'.... [They suggest] that there's some aspect of the psyche that's nonlocal in space and time — immortal, eternal, and omnipresent."

Admittedly, someone who is not open to the idea may not necessarily now feel compelled to conclude he possesses an eternal soul. Still, whether or not one chooses to accept the findings, it should at least be clear that science and rationality do not force one to conclude that death is the end. If anything, the reverse is becoming true nowadays. More and more educated people, thinkers, and scholars are finding it rationally acceptable and even compelling that consciousness persists beyond death.

What is the truth? Is belief in the afterlife nothing more than wishful thinking? Dr. Stevenson's personal conviction is certain enough to state that "the evidence of human survival after death is strong enough to permit a belief in survival on the basis of the evidence."[14] Note that permission to believe is not based merely on wishful thinking or tradition; neither is it permission extended only to those who have had firsthand experience. Rather, it is permission granted to all "on the basis of evidence" — evidence collected by some hard-nosed scientists who measure their words very, very carefully.

Therefore, if you needed permission from the scientific, rationally based worldview to believe in survival beyond bodily death, know that such permission has been granted.

Whether skeptic or believer, this naturally leads to another question: If we do possess a soul that survives bodily death, what happens to us after we die? What do we really know about the journey of the soul after bodily death? To that we turn to the next chapter.

Notes

1. Genesis 2:7.
2. In the 1950s, a young American scientist discovered that stars in rotating spiral galaxies seem to be held together by an unseen force. Vera Rubin proposed the idea that the space between the stars was filled with invisible stuff she called "dark matter." Scientists now believe that dark matter could make up an unbelievable 90 to 99 percent of the universe. Incredibly, in the 1990s scientists began talking about and garnering support for the existence of something even more primary : "dark energy," or quintessence (Kenneth C. Davis, *Don't Know Much about the Universe: Everything You Need to Know about the Cosmos but Never Learned* [New York: HarperCollins, 2001], pp. 304–6; Stephen Hawking and David Filkin, *Stephen Hawking's Universe: The Cosmos Ex-*

plained [Basic Books, 1998], pp. 160, 171–173; Marcia Bartusiak, *Through a Universe Darkly: A Cosmic Tale of Ancient Ethers, Dark Matter, and the Fate of the Universe* [New York: Avon Books, 1993]).

3. Y. M. Tucazinsky, *The Bridge of Life* (Moznaim, 1983), translated from the Hebrew, *Gesher HaChaim* (1949), which was written by Rabbi N. Tucazinsky,
4. Psalms 144:4.
5. For instance, in his *Republic*, Plato detailed the case of a soldier apparently killed in battle but revived before his body was cremated. He related experiences that correspond in many ways to reports of what researchers today call "out-of-body experiences."
6. Pp. 40–42.
7. Cited in "The Evidence of Man's Survival after Death: A Historical and Critical Survey with a Summary of Recent Developments," by Ian Stevenson, M.D., *Journal of Nervous and Mental Disease*, p. 154.
8. Dr. Ian Stevenson writes, "If materialism [the belief that we are no more than our material, physical bodies] were true, telepathy should not occur; but it does occur, so materialism must be false" (*Children Who Remember Past Lives*, p. 228).
9. Arthur Koestler, *The Roots of Coincidence* (Random House, 1972), p. 14.
10. Dr. Stevenson points out, for instance, that despite the fact that "most scientists, and certainly nearly all neuroscientists," believe that what we call "mind" can be explained by the current understanding of the physical brain, the truth is that it is not necessarily so. They may have "begun to show in detail" how the brain and mind are connected and have opti-

mistic hopes that more details will be worked out in the future, but "they assume, in an act of faith, that no other solution to the relationship between brain and mind will be found." Stevenson also writes that what is currently known about brains does not explain consciousness, mental imagery, memory, or telepathy (*Children Who Remember Past Lives*, pp. 225–28).

11. W. Carington, *Telepathy: An Outline of Its Facts, Theory, and Implications* (Methuen, 1945), cited in Stevenson, loc. cit.
12. See his *Life at Death* and *Heading Toward Omega*.
13. Michael Sabom, *Recollections of Death*.
14. "The Evidence of Man's Survival after Death," *Journal of Nervous and Mental Disease*, pp. 167–68. Dr. Stevenson points out that the evidence comes from "not just one type of experience, but from several: apparitions [which we did not discuss], out-of-the-body experiences, deathbed visions [i.e., NDEs], certain kinds of mediumistic communications [which we did not discuss either], and cases of the reincarnation type [which we will discuss in some detail in part 2, 'Past Lives']." Of course, when one also adds evidence mentioned above gathered from studies on extrasensory perception and prayer, the indicators for evidence of survival beyond the grave is even more broadly based. And, finally, even beyond that, Dr. Stevenson notes that "within each of these groups of experiences investigators have recorded not just one or two examples, but many or — for some — hundreds."

Journey of the Soul

> We go through many stages when we're here. We shed a baby body, go into a child's, from a child to an adult, an adult into old age. Why shouldn't we go one step beyond and shed the adult body and go on to a spiritual plane?
>
> Dr. Brian Weiss, *Many Lives, Many Masters*

As explained above, Dr. Raymond Moody was the first researcher to identify not only the existence of near-death experiences but a recurring number of consistent sensations associated with them. As we related, many reported floating above their bodies and watching the impassioned efforts of others to revive them. Others told of traveling through a dark passageway or tunnel. Still others described encounters with beings of light or with an all-encompassing warm, restorative light. Many understood that light to be God. And ultimately there was the life review, the dramatic and sometimes traumatic experience of seeing one's life pass before one's eyes.

In truth, very few individuals experienced all of these sensations. Most had one or two of them at best. Yet these four experiences — out-of-body travel, traveling down a tunnel, encountering light, and life review — are among the most common core near-death experiences reported over and over again.

How does the Torah understanding of life after life compare to Dr. Moody's and other researchers' findings? Before answering that, first a very important disclaimer.

Concepts brought in the more than two thousand pages of the Talmud are only the tip of the iceberg. Typically scholars can spend several months mulling over no more than ten pages of text. Working intensely on one piece for five, ten, even fifteen or more hours per day, they mine every nuance of every word, cross-referencing and comparing it with similar statements in other Talmudic passages, until the full significance of the text becomes clear to them — yet even then they realize that they have barely touched the surface!

The ensuing pages will frequently draw on Talmudic and Talmudic-like texts. It must be borne in mind that, as tempting as it is to believe one understands the concept based on the translation presented here, it is impossible for the uninitiated to grasp the full meaning of the concepts. Why, then, cite the texts? To draw parallels.

That word, *parallel*, is important to understand. Parallel

concepts do not intersect. They are two entirely independent concepts, each emanating from a system unique to it. However, since they are parallel, they obviously share some common features. Therefore, the Talmudic texts brought here are meant only to draw parallels to the near-death experiences as reported by Dr. Moody and others. The intelligent reader will understand that these Talmudic passages only scratch the surface.

Full-fledged comparisons cannot be made for another reason. All the accumulated knowledge of the field of near-death research, which is only in its infancy, is not even like an ant compared to the Empire State Building. Thus, we cannot draw unwarranted comparisons between Talmudic texts, which contain more than appears to the eye, and current research, which is so recent.

That said, we can return to the question: How does the Talmudic understanding of life after life compare to Dr. Moody's and other researchers' findings?

The place to begin is to see if the idea of a near-death experience is found anywhere in the traditional Jewish sources. And the answer to that is yes.

> Rabbi Joseph the son of Rabbi Joshua ben Levi became ill, and his soul left him. When he recovered, his father asked him, "What did you see?"
>
> He replied, "I saw an upside-down world. Those who were on top here [i.e., in terms of status] were below there, and those who were [considered] low here were on top there."

> His father responded, "My son, you have seen a clear world."[1]

How long was Rabbi Joseph dead? Was the upside-down world he saw the same world Raymond Moody's subjects saw? These questions are unanswered. What we do know is that at least fifteen centuries ago the Talmud recorded the incident of a great man who left this world, caught a glimpse of the next world, and returned to tell about it.

There are numerous other parallel cases, not only limited to the Talmud. The Midrash — which, like the Talmud, is a primary source of Jewish teaching but deals less with law and more with ethics and esoterica — comments, for instance, on a verse in the book of Exodus. When Moses asked God to show him His glory, he was told, "Man cannot see Me and live,"[2] from which the Sages of the Midrash inferred, "Man cannot see Me and live; however, when he ceases to live here [i.e., when he dies], he will see Me."[3]

Another *midrash* describes the revelation at Mount Sinai:

> The voice of the first commandment went forth, and the heavens and earth quaked, the waters and rivers fled, the mountains and hills jumped, the great oaks fell flat, the dead in Sheol stood on their feet...[and] the Israelites who were alive [then] fell on their faces and died.[4]

The import is that they died in order to hear the first of the Ten Commandments directly from God. Similarly, the Talmud records:

> Rabbi Joshua ben Levi said: At every word that went forth from the mouth of the Holy One, blessed be He, the souls of Israel departed.... If their souls had departed [i.e., they were dead], how could they hear the second word? The answer is that He...revived them.[5]

From these accounts we can say that the Sages of old understood the revelation at Mount Sinai almost as a collective near-death experience. The people had to die in order to hear the word of God.

The point is simply to draw a parallel between the basic near-death experience as reported in contemporary sources and the understanding of Judaism as it has always existed in the ancient primary sources. To the Jewish Sages of old, death generally led to the direct experience of God. It certainly was not a blank state of being.

Let's now try to find parallels in some of the specifics of the near-death experience.

Notes

1. *Pesachim* 50a.
2. Exodus 33:20
3. *Sifri, Beha'alotcha* 103. Similarly, "The soul does not go out

of the body until it beholds the Divine Presence, as it says, 'For man shall not see Me and live' " (*Pirkei D'Rabbi Eliezer* 34a).

4. *Pirkei D'Rabbi Eliezer* 41; *Bemidbar Rabbah* 14:22.
5. *Shabbat* 88b.

The Out-of-Body Experience

The next thing I knew, I was in a room, crouched in a corner of the ceiling. I could see my body below me.... I could see the doctors and nurses working on me. My doctor was there, and so was Sandy, one of the nurses. I heard Sandy say, "I wish we didn't have to do this." I wondered what they were doing.... I heard a doctor say, "Stand back," and then he pushed a button [which sent an electrical shock through the body].... Suddenly I was back inside my body. One minute I was looking down at my face. I could see the tops of the doctors' heads. After he pushed that button, I was suddenly looking into a doctor's face.

Closer to the Light

Boy, I sure didn't realize that I looked like that! You know, I'm only used to seeing myself in the pic-

> tures or from the front of a mirror, and both of those look flat. But all of a sudden, there I — or my body — was, and I could see it. I could definitely see it, full view, from about five feet away. It took me a few minutes to recognize myself.
>
> *Life After Life*

The out-of-body experience of near-death victims is one of the most commonly reported sensations.

There are a number of explicit Jewish sources that parallel it. The most unique is the constellation of laws and customs surrounding Jewish rites of burial and mourning. One of the explicit statements that reflects ancient Jewish awareness of the out-of-body experience related to death is the following:

> For three days [after death] the soul hovers over the body, intending to reenter it, but as soon as it sees [the] appearance [of its face] change [i.e., noticeable decay begins to set in], it departs....[1]

It may seem obvious to some, but this illustrates conclusively that the out-of-body experience was documented long before Dr. Moody.

But what does it mean to be out of your body? What are you if not your body? An interesting sub-theme of the out-of-body experience reported by some of Dr. Moody's subjects is how they became aware of a "spiritual" body. Dr. Moody relates:

The Out-of-Body Experience

> One NDEr I spoke to several years ago said he studied his hands while he was in this state [i.e., out of body] and saw them to be composed of light with tiny structures in them. He could see the delicate whorls of his fingerprints and the tubes of light up his arms.[2]

This description is particularly fascinating because ancient Jewish mystical writings, principally the Kabbalah, are filled with mentions of the spiritual body, which is likened to a "garment of the soul."[3] And while there is certainly more to the idea than a soul's cosmetic outward appearance, the Kabbalah seems to understand the garment of the soul in a literal sense as well.

> Those who are about to come [down into this world] are dressed with garments — with faces and bodies — like those in this world.... [When they actually enter this world] they take off their spiritual garments and put on the garments of this world.... When it is time for them to leave this world, the garment of the body [is taken off], and they [put back on] the garment that they had to divest themselves of when they entered this world.[4]

The nature of this body, according to the *Zohar*, is ethereal. In fact, the Midrash talks about the "garments of light" Adam wore before his sin, which were exchanged for "garments of skin"[5] after his fall.[6] (*Light* and *skin* are virtually the same word in Hebrew.)

Consequently, according to these sources, the picture arises of human beings endowed with a spiritual body as difficult to describe as a garment of light. We are not necessarily aware of it in this life. Only upon disengaging from our physical raiment is it possible to first become aware of our ethereal garment. Yet we do possess such a garment, and the independent accounts of contemporary NDErs apparently verify this.

The out-of-body experience is often associated with a slow realization that one has died. It does not sink in right away. There is a strange feeling of detachment and even alienation toward the body one has always identified with. Some have remarked that they felt sorry for their lifeless body as if it were someone else's.

This slow realization is reminiscent of the denial of death Dr. Elizabeth Kubler-Ross wrote about concerning the terminally ill[7] — the difference being that denial seems to continue even for the individual who dies! Disembodied consciousness is first perceived by the NDEr as merely a new experience, not death. Before the truth sinks in, it is almost as if one is dreaming the entire experience.

Perhaps this is what another *midrash* means when it says that "the dead man hears his praises [at his eulogy] as in a dream."[8] It does not seem real; it has the surrealism of a dream — at least at the very beginning.

NDE research purports to describe the experience of death, but obviously it covers only the first leg of the journey at best. No one studied has claimed to have been dead for several days. Is the near-death experience identical to the full-death experience? Is the five- or ten-minute experience of death indicative of everything to come?

Regarding the out-of-body component of the experience, Jewish sources suggest the following.

For three days, according to the Talmudic source above, the soul may believe it can somehow reenter its body (perhaps a further indication of the deep psychological need to deny death). According to another source, even after the reality sinks in, the yearning to return to the body does not fully abate. Thus, "all the seven days of mourning the soul goes forth and returns from its home [on earth] to its paradise-like abode and from its paradise-like abode to its [former] home."[9]

From this source it would appear that the disembodied soul has the ability — and desire — to go back and forth between two places: the physical world and the spiritual world. This should not be surprising. We are very attached to our physical bodies, even the more spiritually inclined among us. Despite the paradise-like setting in which the soul may find itself, the soul seeks to return to the place in which it invested so much time and effort: this world. Even NDErs who report reluctance at the prospect of returning to their bodies do, obviously, eventually all return to their bodies. Thus, after separation from the body, our sentiments toward it do not necessarily disappear. Nevertheless, the soul's yearning to return to the place of its physical life usually decreases over time, as the Talmud explains.

While the body is in existence, the soul ascends and descends [between paradise and the physical world]; after twelve months the body decays and the soul ascends and descends no more.[10]

Despite the spiritual nature of the soul, it is very much connected to its body. That's why it hovers above it, even when it no longer makes sense to do so. Yet over time it adjusts to its new reality.

Notes

1. *Vayikra Rabbah* 18.
2. *The Light Beyond*, p. 10.
3. *Zohar* II:150a; cf. *Ramban* (Nachmanides), Genesis 49:3; *Rabbeinu Bachya*, loc. cit, and *Kad HaKemach*, s.v. "*kinah*"; *Sefer HaGilgulim*, ch. 64 and 69.
4. *Zohar* II:150a.
5. As related in Genesis 3:21.
6. *Bereishit Rabbah* 20:12.
7. In her book *On Death and Dying*.
8. *Bereishit Rabbah* 96:24.
9. *Pirkei D'Rabbi Eliezer* 34.
10. *Shabbat* 152b.

The Laws of Mourning and the Out-of-Body Experience

> Better to go to a house of mourning than a house of mirth...for the living will take [the lessons of death] to heart.
>
> *Ecclesiastes 7:2*

> Be fervent in my funeral eulogy, for I will be standing there.
>
> *Shabbat 153a*

Although research into near-death experiences has become part of the public consciousness for some two decades now, it has not necessarily been translated into practical ethics. Admittedly, issues such as separation between church and state and the wide variety of religious customs make it practically, if not ethically, very difficult to do so. Nevertheless, knowledge that the soul survives death has long been framed into a practical, ethical code of behavior in traditional Jewish sources.

Jewish law recognizes three basic stages in the mourning process: the first seven days, called "*shivah*," the first thirty days, and the first year. At the end of each of these intervals, certain restrictions on the mourners are relaxed.

It is fascinating to note that while these stages are certainly intended to aid the grieving process for the close relatives of the deceased, the soul is also going through the grieving process. Thus the Talmud says, "A man's soul mourns for himself seven days."[1] Consequently, the first seven days are particularly important to help the bereaved get over their loss, but this period is at least as important to the deceased. Both are going through the same grieving process!

After seven days, the intensity of the loss the soul experiences decreases, but it is still powerful until the thirtieth day. Finally, "after twelve months the body decays, and the soul ascends and descends no more."[2] The three stages of mourning, then, reflect the metapsychological state of the soul more than the psychological state of the bereaved.

Virtually all of Jewish law on burial and mourning reflects this reality. For instance, another law declares that it is forbidden to leave the room of a person about to die "because the soul is desolate at the time it leaves the body."[3] The departing soul is keenly cognizant of any act of abandonment. It may be out of its body, but it is very much present.

The Laws of Mourning

For this reason, it is a fundamental principle of Jewish law that the living show great respect to a dead body. Thus, upon expiration, the eyes and mouth of the deceased must be closed, and the body must be covered and then buried as quickly as possible — all along handled with the greatest dignity.

Traditionally the task of handling the body has been reserved for a highly esteemed and select group of nonprofit volunteers called the "*chevrah kaddisha*," or the "holy society." (Profit-making funeral homes with persuasive directors coaxing people to spend more and more money for the "honor" of the dead is essentially a new phenomenon to Jews.) Upon the "holy society" falls the responsibility of the *taharah*, to thoroughly wash the dead body, to clothe it in funeral shrouds, to make sure someone is stationed over the body literally every minute until burial — in general to put the family (and the deceased) at ease, knowing that the body is being handled with the highest degree of dignity and sanctity.

Furthermore, whoever handles the body, whether to move it or clean it, has to ask forgiveness: "Please forgive me, So-and-so, the son of So-and-so, for moving or cleaning your body." One is obligated by Jewish law to say this even if no one else is present. Obviously this law makes sense only if it reflects the belief that the soul is hovering and cringes at the sight of any disrespect shown to its body. The Talmud states:

> The dead one knows all that is said in its presence

until the grave is filled in.... [Another opinion:] Until the flesh rots away.[4]

Therefore Jewish law forbids idle or inane chatter in front of the deceased.[5] It is an insult to its dignity, and the soul hears everything. It's even forbidden to say or do anything that might remind the hovering soul that it is no longer capable of fulfilling religious law. This is considered "mocking the impoverished," for Judaism teaches that the dead differ from the living primarily in that they no longer have the free will to serve God. That inability is the greatest impoverishment.

The prohibition of "mocking the impoverished" goes so far as to restrict the outward wearing of the traditional four-cornered garment biblical law requires Jewish men to wear, the *tzitzit*. The Vilna Gaon (who died in 1796), one of the holiest sages in recent Jewish history, reportedly cried on his deathbed. When asked why, he held the strings of the four-cornered garment in his hands and declared, "For a few pennies, one can perform God's commandment in this world. Where I am going, I will not have that luxury." Thus Jewish law obligates the person in the vicinity of the dead to tuck the strings of his four-cornered garment into his pants.

One of the more curious laws is the one that obligates all close relatives of the deceased to tear their garments. In Jewish mystical writings, the body is called a "garment of the soul" (see above, page 53). Tearing one's garment, therefore, may be more than just a symbolic gesture, but a reassurance to the deceased hovering nearby that the bereaved loved one feels the loss as if his or her own body was torn asunder.

Rabbis often decry the custom of tearing a small ribbon instead of an actual garment. It can be construed to imply that the loss of the loved one is not very deep; it merely calls for the tearing of some prefabricated ribbon the rabbi or funeral director hands out. For the grieving soul hovering about, it is a statement that their loss is not worth the price of a new shirt or sport jacket.

It is furthermore reflective of the sterility with which modern society faces death, which Dr. Elizabeth Kubler-Ross[6] and many others have written about so poignantly. Death, they write, is something contemporary society tries to deny, and this is reflective of so many institutional practices. It is not healthy for the grieving party to hide the inevitability of death behind septic, emotionally distant gestures. Certainly for the hovering soul the loss is heartfelt. It is a great service therefore for those close relatives who remain behind to outwardly express their heartfelt grief by tearing their own outer garment as if it were their own body.

It was mentioned above that the dead know everything said in their presence at least until burial. In an even more explicit statement, one Talmudic Sage said to another, "Be fervent in my funeral eulogy, for I will be standing there."[7] The eulogy is more than just a vital component of the grieving process for the bereaved. It is even more important to the deceased. The deceased knows everything said about him. That is the reason a eulogy is not only codified in Jewish law, but that it must be deeply felt and arouse the audience to weep.

This sensitivity to the needs of the soul also explains the propensity Jews have for lighting candles in memory of the deceased. It is more than just to honor their memory.

> The soul derives pleasure from light, for it itself is a portion of the Light. That's why King Solomon compared the soul to a light — "The soul of man is the candle of God" (Proverbs 20:27). Therefore, on the anniversary of the passing of one's parent or other relatives, one kindles a light called the *'yahrtzeit'*...for on this day the soul has permission to travel about the world. It comes to the synagogue and sees the light burning for it and receives spiritual satisfaction from it.[8]

In a similar vein, the custom to put up a monument is no mere custom. The Jewish sages actually called the monument "*nefesh*," which means "soul."[9] The idea is that even long after the body is buried and the soul has found respite in the afterlife, a residue of its soul remains permanently attached to the spot where it was buried. The monument, therefore, is not just for the bereaved, but also for the deceased.[10]

Helping to ensure that a deceased person receives a proper burial is viewed as one of the most meritorious

The Laws of Mourning

deeds in all of Jewish law. Treating the body with dignity is an act of altruism, made purer by the fact that it is performed without the expectation of a favor in return. The altruism, however, is not toward the lifeless body but toward the hovering soul, which is very aware of how its body is being treated. The dead may be helpless, but they very much depend on the living to help them.

For that reason various mourner's prayers have become part of the thrice-daily Jewish prayer service. Through these prayers — above all the Kaddish — the soul of the departed can become elevated.

This is an important principle. Normally it is understood that death freezes the soul at whatever spiritual level it is at. However, Kaddish — which is a prayer, not about death, but rather about the affirmation of God's greatness — is seen as a way for children to perform a righteous deed in the merit of their parents, raising their parents' status in the world beyond. (The righteous deed in this case is leading a multitude of people in a public declaration of God's greatness.) Kaddish, like other prayers (the *Yizkor* prayer recited on Jewish holidays and the *Keil Malei Rachamim* prayer), charity, and Torah study are viewed in Jewish law as tools by which the living can help the deceased, who are no longer capable of helping themselves. Thus, it is among the greatest and purest acts of altruism one can perform.

The bottom line is that if the out-of-body experience is authentic, it sheds an entirely different light on the way one should mourn. Modern society traditionally views the funeral as a ritual for the sake of the bereaved. Jewish law, on the other hand, reflects the understanding that the grieving process must be carried out above all else with a sensitivity to the deceased. The surviving loved ones perform a great service by attending to the needs of their departed with dignity and expressing their loss with outward manifestations.

Conversely, relatives of the deceased, and those who aid them, potentially do a great disservice if they are ignorant of the fact that the actual consciousness of the departed may be hovering over every minute detail concerning the very proceedings of its funeral and thereafter. If the deceased knows everything said in its presence and all that is done to its body, it is vitally important information for all to know. Certainly that has been the assumption of Jewish law as reflected in the burial and mourning obligations.

The out-of-body experience, then, is not only known in Jewish writings, but that knowledge has long been acted upon.

Let's move on to the next basic component of the core near-death experience.

Notes

1. *Shabbat* 152a.
2. Ibid.
3. *Shulchan Aruch*, *Yoreh Deah* 339:4, and *Taz* 3.
4. *Shabbat* 152b.
5. *Berachot* 3b.

6. In her book *Death and Dying*.
7. *Shabbat* 153a.
8. Cited in *Mourning in Halacha*, p. 414.
9. *Talmud Yerushalmi, Ta'anit*, ch. 2.
10. "The holy *Zohar* and the writings of the Arizal explain that...the *nefesh* [as opposed to the *ruach* and *neshamah*, other soul components] remains constantly hovering over the grave.... In honor of the *nefesh*, in order to give it a defined place to dwell, we mark the grave or build a structure over it..." (*Ta'amei HaMinhagim*, p. 476, cited in *Mourning in Halacha* 41:1).

The Tunnel

> I heard the doctors say that I was dead, and that's when I began to feel as though I were tumbling, actually kind of floating, through this blackness, which was some kind of enclosure. There are not really words to describe this. Everything was very black, except that, way off from me, I could see this light. It was a very, very brilliant light, but not too large at first. It grew larger as I came nearer and nearer to it.
>
> *Life After Life*

It has been described alternatively as a tunnel, a tube, a pipe, an enclosure, a cave, a valley, even a stairway or doorway. According to Dr. Moody, it "generally happens after body separation."[1] It's like a cosmic ride to a different dimension.

There are generally different components to this experience:

The Tunnel

- the initial sensation, often associated with a noise,
- traveling down the passageway itself, and
- the perception of a light at the end of the tunnel.

Let's take each component one at a time. One NDEr reported:

> I [heard] this ringing noise: *brrrrrnnnng...brrrrrnnnng...brrrrrrnnnnng....*[2]

Another NDEr:

> [I heard] a buzzing sound.[3]

And yet another:

> Suddenly I heard a whooshing sound in my ears.[4]

Dr. Moody has written that he also heard it described as a "loud click, a roaring, a banging, and a whistling sound, like the wind."[5] Those are the words of people living in the twentieth century. Centuries beforehand, however, the following teaching was canonized in a *midrash*:

> What is implied by "the soul is not filled" (Ecclesiastes 6:6)? It implies that at the time of death the soul does not leave the body smoothly. How does the soul depart?... Like the sound of rushing waters.... Alternatively, like the sound of gushing waters from a canal.[6]

The descriptions are remarkably similar. A *whoosh* can easily be explained as a rushing sound, like gushing waters. However, even if some of the particular descriptions differ, the mere fact that the first sensation is some kind of sound draws the correlation. The separation of body and soul seems to officially begin with an auditory sensation.

The second component of the tunnel experience, the actual traveling down the tunnel itself, does not necessarily have to be a tunnel. It can be a doorway or a valley. It's interesting to note that one of the common descriptions is that of a cave, because the *Zohar* writes that the "entranceway into paradise" is the cave described in Genesis where Abraham buried Sarah, which is situated in Hebron.[7] Furthermore, states the *Zohar*, people travel through this cave when they pass out of this world![8] (That, of course, does not necessarily mean that everyone who describes the experience as going through a cave goes through Hebron, but again the parallel is striking.)

Even more intriguing is the *Zohar*'s inclusion of a fact that might have gone unnoticed had we not been looking for it. After Abraham entered the cave to inspect it, he saw "a door open to paradise," and, "moreover, he saw a shining light that lit up the cave." This is part 3 of our tunnel experience, the perception of a light somewhere in the darkness.

In addition to the cave description, Dr. Moody reports that more than one subject perceived the dark passageway as a valley, to which that subject added, "Well, now I know what the Bible means by 'the valley of the shadow of death,' because I've been there."[9]

The comparison is apt. King David in the famous psalm is talking about his total faith in the Shepherd Who he knows is with him though he cannot see Him, in spite of the fact that he is presently immersed in the deepest of darknesses, the loneliest of lonelinesses.[10] Similarly, the NDErs report, the tunnel is a separation between themselves and God (or heaven or their perception of paradise). Death is all around, and they are more alone than they have ever been, yet they are strangely comforted; they are confident that there is literally a light at the end of the tunnel.

It should be mentioned that the experience of light at the end of the tunnel is often substituted in the accounts of contemporary NDErs by a vision of lush fields and other beautiful pastoral scenes. On that theme, note that David, at the beginning of the psalm, writes how the watchful Shepherd "lays me down in green pastures and leads me beside tranquil waters."[11] That knowledge gives him the fortitude to walk through the valley of the shadow of death with confidence and tranquillity. It is the comforting paradise that awaits him upon passage through the valley.

There is still one major question. What exactly does the tunnel experience represent? What part does it play in the journey of the soul?

To answer that, the *Zohar*'s statement that this passageway is situated in Hebron, "the entrance to paradise," is most enlightening. The root meaning of Hebron in Hebrew, *chevron*, is "join." Thus its name is descriptive of the place where heaven "joins" earth. In fact, the mere description of it as a doorway implies that it serves as a dividing line, a link, between two realms.

The tunnel experience, then, is apparently the passageway separating this realm and the next. It is the twilight zone between heaven and earth, if you will. And that seems to sum up the many and varied adjectives NDErs use to describe this leg of the experience. Each is trying to explain some type of passage through a connecting point between two entirely different realms.

Notes

1. *The Light Beyond*, p. 11.
2. *Life After Life*, p. 31.
3. *Closer to the Light*, p. 28.
4. Ibid.
5. *Life After Life*, p. 30.
6. *Kohelet Rabbah* 6:6.
7. *Zohar* 1:127a.
8. Ibid.
9. *Life After Life*, p. 34.
10. Psalm 23.
11. Psalms 23:2.

The Light

> I then entered a dark round tube or hole. I could call it a tunnel. I seemed to go headfirst through this thing and suddenly was in a place filled up with love and a beautiful white light. The place seemed holy. Plants and flowers. I could see beautiful scenes. As I walked through this meadow I saw people.... One was my father, who had died two years before. He looked radiant. He looked happier than I had ever seen him before and much younger. My grandmothers and grandfathers were there, too.
>
> *Transformed by the Light*

Usually after exiting the tunnel many NDErs report seeing beings of light. This in itself is a parallel, for King Solomon compared the soul to a candle of God.[1] Also, as mentioned above, Adam before his fall is described as wearing a garment of light (page 53 above). And the prophet Daniel wrote, "Those who are wise will shine as the brightness of the firmament."[2] Medieval Jewish commentators described the soul as "luminous like light."[3] The bottom line is that whoever the beings of light are, the fact that they are described as radiating intensely bright light is what one would expect given the traditional sources.

Not surprisingly, some identify those beings as family and loved ones. The identification of family members as the beings who greet one after death draws a parallel to the verse in the Bible that describes death as a time when one is "gathered to your people."[4] In an even more explicit statement, another verse says, "Therefore, behold, I will gather you to your fathers, and you shall be gathered to your graves in peace."[5] Regarding those verses, the Midrash states explicitly:

> All souls go forth [after death] and are gathered, each one's soul to the generation of his father's and to his people.... When the soul goes forth from the body, then the righteous come to meet them and say, "Come unto Peace."[6]

Often the NDEr is not able to identify any particular being of light, but nevertheless feels a definite "presence." Interestingly, the same *midrash* above relates that expiring souls encounter the *Shechinah*, literally, "the [Divine] Presence." Even so, NDErs vary widely as to the definition of who or what that Presence is. Many Christians identify it as their savior. That obviously presents theological problems for Jews and others. On the other hand, leading NDE researcher Kenneth Ring writes, "[In all of my years of research into NDEs] I cannot recall even one instance in which the being of light was said to have identified himself as Jesus."[7]

Dr. Melvin Morse dealt with a similar problem when one of his NDE subjects identified the being of light as none other than Elvis Presley(!), who said to her, "Hi, Bev, do you remember me?"[8] Dr. Morse also cites reports of NDErs from Africa who similarly made identifications specific to their culture. However, both he and Dr. Ring conclude that all such discrepancies do not reflect differences in the essential core experience. Dr. Morse therefore understands the vision of Elvis to be typical of an "embellishment," an identification that — notwithstanding the fact that it is very real to the NDEr — emanates from within the person and is based on his or her cultural experience.[9]

The idea of embellishment upon an essentially truthful otherworldly vision has a parallel in Jewish sources. According to Rabbi Moshe Chaim Luzzatto, an apprentice prophet might misinterpret a genuine prophetic experience and state a false idea that was not intended to be conveyed.[10] That is why all genuine prophets needed a master to guide them through the many pitfalls inherent in obtaining an unambiguous understanding of the celestial world.

Similarly, the Talmud reports that when the four greatest Sages of their day endeavored to enter the highest chambers of the divine mystery they warned each other beforehand of the extreme dangers of misidentifying the visions they were about to behold.[11]

If embellishment was a concern of those specifically trained to view the spiritual world, it certainly has to be considered a factor for the NDEr who obtains that view through the unexpected circumstances of his near death. Still, the core experience, as the above researchers conclude, can be considered authentic. In its most generic form, the light experience often begins with encounters with one or several beings of light. Of course, it cannot be denied that the most powerful NDEs lead the beholder to conclude that the light they have seen is none other that the Light of God, or at least their perception of God. Not surprisingly, then, if one literally "sees the light," he or she is invariably changed forevermore.[12]

> The next thing I knew...I was standing in a mist, and I knew immediately that I had died.... The mist started being infiltrated with enormous light, and the light just got brighter and brighter and brighter, and it is so bright but it doesn't hurt your eyes, but it's brighter than anything you've ever encountered in your whole life.
>
> At that point, I had no consciousness anymore of having a body. It was just pure consciousness. And this enormously bright light seemed to cradle

me. I just seemed to exist in it and be part of it and be nurtured by it, and the feeling just became more and more and more ecstatic and glorious and perfect. And everything about it was...if you took the one thousand best things that ever happened to you in your life and multiplied by a million, maybe you could get close to that feeling. I don't know. But you're just engulfed by it, and you begin to know a lot of things.

I remember I knew that everything, everywhere in the universe was OK, that the plan was perfect. That whatever was happening — the wars, famine, whatever — was OK. Everything was perfect....

And the whole time I was in that state...I was just an infinite being...knowing that...you're home forever. That you're safe forever. And that everybody else was.[13]

The light seen by this and many NDErs is obviously not like the light we experience in this world. It shares basic qualities, but it is much more. Similarly, in Jewish sources the light we experience in this world is only a minor reflection of the light that awaits us in the hereafter:

> With the light that God created on the first day one could see from one end of the universe to the other. However, as soon as God beheld the [future] corruptness of the generation of the flood and the

generation of the Tower [of Babel], He acted and hid [the light] from them.... And for whom did He reserve it? For the righteous in the hereafter.[14]

The light of the first day of Creation — the light of "And God said, 'Let there be light'"[15] — is obviously an unusual light to begin with, since it existed before the creation of the sun and stars (which took place on the fourth day). It is therefore understood by Jewish sources as primarily representative of a spiritual light. More, this spiritual light represents wisdom above anything else. Thus, commentators explain that the expression "seeing from one end of the universe to the other" is a way of describing the ability to grasp any and all knowledge, a way of having the doors to the entire universe swung wide open.

Significant in this Talmudic teaching is the statement that this light cannot be perceived in this world. It exists exclusively in the domain of the hereafter. The picture that emerges, then, is that upon death a person will encounter the light, which gives him absolute access to all wisdom, and if that person is worthy, he will bask in the light eternally. In this regard, the ancient Talmudic picture and the description of contemporary NDErs are clearly parallel.

Another point beckoning mention from the NDE described above is the striking resemblance of the statement "If you took the one thousand best things that ever happened to you in your life and multiplied by a million, maybe you could get close to that feeling" with the following Talmudic aphorism: "Better one moment of pleasure in the hereafter than all the pleasures of this world."[16]

Regarding this aphorism, a Jewish scholar of note explained: If you took all the happiest moments in your past and added to that all the happiest moments in your future, and added to that all the happiest moments of your neighbor's life, and added to that all the happiest moments of each member of your community's life, and added to that all the happiest moments of each member of your generation's life, and added to that all the happiest moments of every human being who has ever lived and who will ever live — even then you would not approach the pleasure of one moment in the hereafter.[17]

The latter part of that Talmudic aphorism is relevant as well: "Better one moment of self-improvement and good deeds in this world than all the life in the hereafter." In other words, while the pleasure of the light in the next world is unsurpassable — indeed, unimaginable — one does not have the opportunity to effect change in oneself there as one does in this world.

This feeling is corroborated by most NDErs, one of whom put it best when she said, "I know that life is for living and that light is for later."[18] In fact, contrary to what one might think, even though studies show that NDErs generally lose their fear of death, most are "mentally healthier than before their experience...[and are in no] particular hurry" to die.[19] People who had NDEs as a result of suicide almost never try to kill themselves again, while those who did not have an NDE after attempting suicide have a very high repeat rate.[20]

Thus the Talmudic aphorism bears out in contemporary experience: although there is no pleasure like the light in the afterlife, a well-grounded human being realizes that this life presents opportunities unlike anything else. We experience the light of the hereafter to the degree we work on ourselves in this life. Or, to use the beautiful imagery of the Psalmist, "Light is sown for the righteous...[and will sprout according to how well they cultivated themselves in this life]."[21]

Notes

1. Proverbs 20:27.
2. Daniel 12:3.
3. Rabbi Sa'adiah Gaon being the earliest in his *Emunot V'De'ot* 6:3.
4. Numbers 27:13; Deuteronomy 32:50; see Appendix A, "Afterlife in Scripture."
5. II Kings 22:20; II Chronicles 34:28.
6. *Pirkei D'Rabbi Eliezer* 34a.
7. *Heading Toward Omega*, p. 87.
8. *Transformed by the Light*, p. 110.
9. Ibid., pp. 119–22; *Heading Toward Omega*, p. 48.
10. *Derech Hashem* 3:4:8–11.
11. *Chagigah* 14b.
12. Interestingly, Dr. Melvin Morse, in his book *Transformed by the Light*, linked the life and personality transformation of

NDErs to one particular component of the NDE: the experience of seeing the light. What is particularly interesting is that some of Dr. Morse's study subjects included patients who had had such an experience without dying. They seemed to have seen the same restorative light while in a dream or altered state. The interesting part of this finding is that these people were changed just as much as those who had seen the light as the result of an NDE. It was not so much the dying that was transformational as the powerful experience of basking in that light.

In a similar vein, Catherine, in Dr. Weiss's *Many Lives, Many Masters*, says in an altered state that the light is "like starting over.... It's a rebirth." she also relates that it's possible for people in physical form to experience the light through their minds. "You can renew through visualizations in hypnosis to help and heal patients."

13. *Heading Toward Omega*, pp. 61–62.
14. *Chagigah* 12a.
15. Genesis 1:3.
16. *Avot* 4:29.
17. Rabbi Eliyahu Dessler, in his *Michtav MeEliyahu*; see the introduction to volume 1 of the English version entitled *Strive for Truth* (Feldheim Publishers).
18. *Transformed by the Light*, p. 27.
19. *The Light Beyond*, p. 40; cf. *Transformed by the Light*, pp. 58–60, 225.
20. "Almost none of the NDErs attempt to kill themselves again" (*The Light Beyond*, p. 99; see also *Closer to the Light*, pp. 184–91).
21. Psalms 97:11.

The Life Review

It was like I knew everything that was stored in my brain. Everything I'd ever known about from the beginning of my life I immediately knew about. And also what was kind of scary was that I knew everybody else in the room knew I knew and that there was no hiding anything — the good times, the bad times, everything.... I had a total clear knowledge of everything.... I realized that there are things that every person is sent to earth to realize and to learn.... Every single thing that you do in your life is recorded and that even though you pass it by, not thinking at the time, it always comes up later. For instance, you may be...at a stoplight and you're in a hurry and the lady in front of you, when the light turns green, doesn't take right off, [she] doesn't notice the light, and you get upset and start honking your horn and telling [her] to hurry up.

The Life Review

> Those are the little kind of things that are recorded that you don't realize at the time are really important.
>
> *Heading Toward Omega*

According to the Talmudic Sages, "All of a person's deeds are written in a book."[1] It is also taught, "Do not think that the grave will be a refuge for you.... In the hereafter you will have to give an account of all your actions before the King of kings...."[2] Furthermore, a person should not think that minor events will be overlooked, for even the deeds a person "tramples beneath his heel [i.e., disregards as of little or no importance] will be brought up for judgment."[3]

It sounds scary.

Well, yes, according to Torah sources, the judgment or life review contains the general air of awe and seriousness that the above NDEr and others relate. There is no sense trying to sugarcoat or diminish the magnitude of the event. On the other hand, the often-stereotyped image of stern patriarchal authoritarian judges spewing fire and brimstone upon sinners in a punitive, almost sadistic fashion is not the image that arises from the primary Torah sources.

Among the proofs is the Talmudic conception of Hell, called "Gehinnom." Gehinnom is a twelve-month period, after which all but the most obdurate evildoers are allowed to enter paradise.[4] Clearly, then, the final "life review" is not perceived as a punitory experience, but as one intended to cleanse and improve; it is an experience that is part of the process of preparing the soul for the ultimate existence.

Judgment is not usually viewed in a positive light in contemporary society. However, sobering up to the reality of a situation, no matter how painful, can truly be liberating. To quote another NDEr:

> Years and years of intense psychoanalysis of the most intense type of external therapy could not have brought me through what I was experiencing rapidly.[5]

And another:

> The most important thing I learned from this experience was that I am responsible for everything I do. Excuses and avoidance were impossible when I was...reviewing my life. And not only that, I saw that responsibility is not bad in the least.... It's funny, but my failings have become very dear to me in a way, because they are my failings, and...I am going to learn from them.... Everything you have done is there [in the review] for you to evaluate, and as unpleasant as some parts of it are for you to see, it feels so good to get it all out.... When I was there in that review, there was no covering up. I was the very people that I hurt, and I was the very people I helped to feel good. I wish I could find some way to convey to everyone how good it feels to know that you are responsible.... It is the most liberated feeling in the world.[6]

Similarly, the goal of divine judgment in the eyes of the Torah is improvement, not "reprovement." Judgment after death is primarily a liberating experience. It allows the soul to purge itself of negative influences.[7]

It's interesting to note, then, that the root of the Hebrew word for rebuke, *tochachah*, means "prove." The idea is that the person's shortcoming is "proved" to him beyond the shadow of a doubt. It is not rebuke in the sense of "Repent ye sinners!" It's more the art — preferably the gentle art — of showing someone the fallacy of his ways for the purpose of his general improvement.[8]

The best type of reproof is the type that allows the individual to come to the conclusion on his or her own. This is why, on the question "Who testifies [at one's judgment after death]?" the Talmud answers, "A person's own soul."[9] Judgment must come from within if it is worth anything. Ultimately the person himself is the judge of his actions and therefore the first to admit to the truth of the information brought to fore. Thus, the Talmud teaches:

> When a person departs to his eternal home, all his deeds are enumerated before him, and he is told, "You have done such-and-such in such-and-such place on such-and-such day." And he replies, "Yes." They say to him, "Sign." And he signs...and, even more so, he acknowledges the justice of the verdict and says, "You have judged me well...."[10]

To understand the process more deeply, it's necessary

to realize the full import of the statement that one's soul testifies at one's judgment. Amplifying this point, Rabbi Aryeh Kaplan, in his fascinating essay, "Immortality and the Soul,"[11] cites philosopher Henri Bergson's suggestion that one of the main functions of the brain is to eliminate activity and awareness rather than produce it. It serves as a type of radar-jamming device for all the sensations and memories that would otherwise overwhelm us if allowed to pour into our minds at once. The brain is thus a kind of "reducing valve." With this understanding, imagine the experience of death, writes Rabbi Kaplan:

> Imagine standing naked before God, with your memory wide open, completely transparent without any jamming mechanism or reducing valve to diminish its force. You will remember everything you ever did.... The memory of every good deed would be the sublimest of pleasures.... But your memory will also be open to all the things of which you are ashamed. They cannot be rationalized away or dismissed. You will be facing yourself, fully aware of the consequences of all your deeds. We all know the terrible shame and humiliation when one is caught in the act of doing something wrong. Imagine being caught by one's own memory with no place to escape....

The life-review process, then, is not a removed reward or punishment, but rather a cause-and-effect showing of a person's life. Whatever a person does good will be experienced as good. Whatever a person does bad will be experienced as bad. Those feelings not only persist, but are magnified after death. And it is these deeds that constitute the essential heaven and hell, happiness and shame, which characterize the basic Torah idea of reward and punishment in the afterlife.

What does the Torah prescribe for one whose soul is stacked with the memories of numerous shameful experiences (as all of us are, for the Torah teaches, "There is no person who lives and does not do some wrong"[12])? Without going into the numerous details, the essence of the idea is simple: sober up to the reality while in this life. Don't wait for the final life review to get out all your garbage. Do it now while you can. After all, even in the afterlife it all comes from you anyway, only there you do not have the same ability to change yourself.

It is a Torah axiom that God is benevolent. "A world of kindness He built."[13] He wants only our good. In fact, the entire purpose of our creation is that we receive the pleasure of basking in His light, in His presence.[14] The greatest gift, though, is to give us the ability to earn that pleasure through our actions. Hence, free will. Hence, wrong choices. However, since God is benevolent, "He does not rejoice in the punishment of the wicked."[15] That's not His purpose. Thus, according to the Torah, until the moment one dies, one always has the option to change.

The dynamic of eradicating the bad and changing oneself in this life is called "*teshuvah*." Although often translated as "repentance," the term literally means "return," as in one who has returned to one's senses, as in one who has returned to one's true self. That return is always sobering and sometimes even painful. Yet true return to the root of one's being actually purges the videotape of the negative act in one's head. It wipes it clean. Therefore, the Sages taught, "Better to suffer shame in this world than in the World to Come,"[16] and, "Blessed is God, Who gave humankind the opportunity to feel shame in this world rather than the next."[17] Cleansed of the negative, all that remains is the positive. And it's those positive acts that constitute the joy of the life everlasting.

The pleasure of a good deed speaks for itself. Dr. Moody tells the story of the NDEr experiencing a life review who suddenly was flashed the memory of the time she found a little girl lost in a department store. The girl was crying and the woman set her upon a counter and talked to her until her mother arrived. In her life review, the pleasure of that memory was unsurpassed.[18]

To conclude, and tie everything together, there is a parable told by one of the latter century's preeminent sages, Rabbi Yisrael Meir HaKohen, known as the Chafetz Chaim:

> A wealthy man was summoned to the palace of the king. In those days, a summons was almost assuredly a bad sign; the person was in trouble with the authorities. It was then that the man found out

who is true friends were. Some "friends" immediately took leave of him upon receipt of the bad news. "You're the one in trouble," they said. "We don't want any part of it."

Others said, "We'll accompany you to the palace. However, we can't go any further. Once we come to the palace gate, we will not be allowed to continue. Sorry."

Thus the man had to enter the palace grounds alone. As he entered the gates, his heart heavy with worry and fear, to his surprise a man was standing at the entrance who said, "I know who you are and why you were summoned." The stranger continued, "Furthermore, I know exactly what needs to be said on your behalf before the king. Have no fear. I will personally escort you into the king's chamber and speak on your behalf, so you have nothing to worry about."

That's what happens when we die, when we are suddenly and unexpectedly summoned to the palace of the King of kings. The first set of friends, who want no part of us, are our material possessions — our money, our status, our political connections. None of it has any meaning over there. And that's the first thing you realize when you reflect soberly upon your death: how insubstantial over there are the things you considered valuable in this world.

The next set of friends who accompany us to the gate are our family and friends. They arrange the funeral. They accompany the body to the grave. But they can go no further. They're not allowed to proceed with you through the palace gate. And so the person finds himself abandoned again.

There is, however, a stranger waiting at the palace entrance who promises to speak for us in the presence of the King. Who is he, this stranger we do not recognize?

He is our good deeds.[19]

The only possession you take with you when you're summoned before the King of kings is the legacy of your life. A life of altruism, kindness, and spiritual yearning will speak for itself. A life spent in pursuit of temporal material possessions that give one a false sense of security is reason to tremble when the day arrives to present yourself before the King.

Notes

1. *Avot* 2:1.
2. Ibid. 4:29.
3. *Avodah Zarah* 18a.
4. *Eiduyot* 2:10.
5. *Heading Toward Omega*, p. 106.
6. *The Light Beyond*, pp. 46–47.
7. It is written, "God is good to all; His love is on His works"

(Psalms 145:9), and, "Your rod and staff comfort me" (ibid. 23:5). A shepherd's staff is a symbol of comfort. When a sheep feels lost or afraid, it looks for the staff towering high above the head of his shepherd. When it sees the staff, it knows that help is nearby. The shepherd's rod, on the other hand, is used to keep the sheep in line. If a sheep wanders off the path, the shepherd hits it with the rod. King David, however, says that both the staff *and rod* comfort him. How can he consider the rod a symbol of comfort? Because King David learns from the rod that God, his Shepherd, still cares enough to correct him and not let him stray. For more on how divine judgment is meant for improvement and for the good of the one being judged, see chapter 18 (especially paragraphs 38–46) of *The Handbook of Jewish Thought*, vol. 2, by Rabbi Aryeh Kaplan (Moznaim, 1992).

8. The classic example of rebuke, according to the Midrash, is Joseph's words to his brothers, "I am Joseph" (Genesis 45:3). It is explained that, not realizing the Egyptian monarch was the brother they had sold into slavery years before, they argued that he release their captive brother Benjamin on the reasoning that not to do so would literally kill their father back in Canaan. To that he answered, "I am Joseph. Is my father still alive?" (ibid.). The implication was "I am Joseph. Did you worry about our father when you sold me into slavery? Where was your concern then"? "And his brothers could not answer him" (ibid.). He had turned their own reasoning against them with the simple words "I am Joseph. Is my father still alive?"

This encapsulates the essence of the Torah idea of *tochachah*, reproof, "proving" to the person the wrongness

of his ways, not verbal castigation (cf. *Beit HaLevi*).
9. *Ta'anit* 11a.
10. Ibid.
11. In *If You Were God: Three Works by Aryeh Kaplan*, pp. 23–37.
12. Ecclesiastes 7:20.
13. Psalms 89:3.
14. *Mesilat Yesharim*, ch. 1.
15. *Megillah* 10b; *Sanhedrin* 39b.
16. *Kiddushin* 81a.
17. *Yevamot* 105b.
18. *Life After Life*, p. 48.
19. This parable appears in *Pirkei D'Rabbi Eliezer*, ch. 34.

PAST LIVES

Reincarnation and Jewish Tradition

> Every soul of Israel needs to be reincarnated many times in order to fulfill all 613 commandments of the Torah in thought, speech, and action.
>
> *Tanya, Iggeret HaKodesh 7, 29*

The word *eschatology* is defined in the dictionary as "a branch of theology concerned with the final events of the history of the world." In truth, eschatology is not exclusively the domain of religion. The most striking example of a secular eschatology would be Marxism: the convulsions and agonies of the class war, its evils resolving themselves into a classless society, the withering of the state, and the blissful existence ever after.

Jewish eschatology is made up of three basic parts:

- the era of the Messiah,
- the afterlife, and
- the World of Resurrection.

The Messiah, according to traditional Jewish sources, will be a human being born of flesh-and-blood parents,[1] unlike the Christian idea, which has him as the son of God conceived immaculately. In fact, Maimonides writes that the Messiah will complete his job and then die like everyone else.[2]

What's his job? To end the agony of exile and usher in a new era of bliss for humanity at large.[3] The time period in which he emerges and completes his task is called the era of the Messiah (or the Messianic era). According to one Talmudic opinion, it's not an era of overt miracles, where the rules of nature are overturned. Rather, the only new element introduced to the world will be peace among the nations, with the Jewish people reigning in their land, unencumbered by persecution and anti-Semitism, free to pursue their spiritual goals like never before.[4]

The afterlife proper is called in the traditional sources *Olam Haba*, or the World to Come. However, the same term, *Olam Haba*, is also used to refer to the renewed utopian world of the future — the *Olam HaTechiyah*, the Resurrected World or World of Resurrection.[5] The former is the place where righteous souls go after death, and they have been going there since the first death. That place is also sometimes called the *Olam HaNeshamot*, the World of

Souls.[6] It's a place where souls exist in a disembodied state, enjoying the pleasure of closeness to God. Thus, genuine near-death experiences are presumably glimpses into the World of Souls, the place most people think of when the term *afterlife* is mentioned.

The World of Resurrection, by contrast, "no eye has seen," as the Talmud states.[7] It's a world, according to most authorities, where the body and soul are reunited to live eternally in a truly perfected state. That world will first come into being only after the Messiah arrives and will be initiated by an event known as the "Great Day of Judgment."[8] The World of Resurrection is thus the ultimate reward, a place where the body will become eternal and spiritual, while the soul will become even more so.[9]

In comparison to a concept like the World to Come, reincarnation is not, technically speaking, a true eschatology. Reincarnation is merely a vehicle toward attaining an eschatological end. It is the reentry of the soul in an entirely new body to the present world. Resurrection, by contrast, is the reunification of the soul with the former body (newly reconstituted) in the World to Come, a world history has not yet witnessed.

Resurrection is thus a pure eschatological concept. Its purpose is to reward the body with eternity and the soul with higher perfection.[10] The purpose of reincarnation is generally twofold: either to make up for a failure in a previous life or to create a new, higher state of personal perfection not previously attained.[11] Resurrection is thus a time of reward; reincarnation a time of repair. Resurrection is a time of reaping; reincarnation a time of sowing.

The fact that reincarnation is part of Jewish tradition comes as a surprise to many people.[12] It is mentioned in numerous places throughout the classical texts of Jewish mysticism, starting with the preeminent sourcebook of Kabbalah, the *Zohar*:[13]

> As long as a person is unsuccessful in his purpose in this world, the Holy One, blessed be He, uproots him and replants him over and over again.[14]
>
> All souls are subject to reincarnation. People do not know the ways of the Holy One, blessed be He! They do not know that they are brought before the tribunal both before they enter this world and after they leave it. They are ignorant of the many reincarnations and secret works they have to undergo and of the number of naked souls and how many naked spirits roam about in the other world without being able to enter within the veil of the King's palace. Men do not know how the souls revolve like a stone that is thrown from a sling. But the time is at hand when these mysteries will be disclosed.[15]

The *Zohar* and related literature are filled with references to reincarnation,[16] addressing questions such as which body is resurrected and what happens to those bodies that did not achieve final perfection,[17] how many chances is a soul given to achieve completion through reincarnation,[18] whether a husband and wife can reincarnate together,[19] if a delay in burial can affect reincarnation,[20] and if a soul can reincarnate into an animal.[21]

The *Bahir*, attributed to the first-century sage Nechuniah ben HaKanah, used reincarnation to address the classic question of why bad things happen to good people and vice versa:

> Why is there a righteous person to whom good things happen, while [another] righteous person has bad things happen to him? This is because the [latter] righteous person did bad in a previous [life] and is now experiencing the consequences.... What is this like? A person planted a vineyard and hoped to grow grapes, but instead sour grapes grew. He saw that his planting and harvest were not successful, so he tore it out. He cleaned out the sour-grape vines and planted again. When he saw that his planting was not successful, he tore it up and planted it again.[22]

Reincarnation is cited by authoritative classic biblical commentators, including the Ramban,[23] Menachem Recanti,[24] and Rabbeinu Bachya.[25] Among the many volumes of the holy Rabbi Yitzchak Luria, known as the "Ari,"[26] most of which come down to us from the pen of his primary disciple, Rabbi Chaim Vital, are profound insights explaining issues related to reincarnation. Indeed, his *Sha'ar HaGilgulim* (The Gates of Reincarnation) is a book devoted exclusively to the subject,[27] including details regarding the soul roots of many biblical personalities and their incarnations from the times of the Bible down to the Ari.

The Ari's teachings and systems of viewing the world spread like wildfire after his death throughout the Jewish world in Europe and the Middle East. If reincarnation had been generally accepted by Jewish intelligentsia beforehand, it became part of the fabric of Jewish scholarship after the Ari's death, inhabiting the thoughts and writings of great scholars and leaders, from classic commentators on the Talmud (for example, the Maharsha, Rabbi Moshe Eidels[28]) to the founder of the chassidic movement, the Ba'al Shem Tov, and the leader of the non-chassidic world, the Vilna Gaon.[29]

The trend continues to this day. Even some of the greatest authorities who are not necessarily known for their mystical bent assume reincarnation to be an accepted basic tenet.[30]

One of the texts the mystics like to cite as a scriptural allusion to the principle of reincarnation is the following verse in the book of Job:

> Behold, all these things does God do — twice, even three times with a man — to bring his soul back from the pit that he may be enlightened with the light of the living.[31]

In other words, God will allow a person to come back

to the world "of the living" from "the pit" (one of the classic biblical terms for Gehinnom) a second and even a third time or more. Generally speaking, however, this verse and others are understood by mystics as mere allusions to the concept of reincarnation. The true authority for the concept is rooted in the tradition.

Until recently, tradition was the only place one could find a basis for the idea of reincarnation. In the past few decades, the idea began trickling into some of the otherwise spiritually sterilized corners of Western society. Although many of these tricklings smelled of hoax and chicanery, some had more legitimacy than others, enough to cause some highly educated and rational scientists to rethink their views about the nature of reality. One of the more poignant examples is the experience of a highly accredited psychiatrist who once considered himself "the original skeptic."

Notes

1. Maimonides, *Mishnah Torah, Hilchot Melachim* 11:3.
2. Commentary to the Mishnah, *Sanhedrin* 10:1; cf. *Sanhedrin* 99a.
3. Maimonides, *Mishnah Torah, Hilchot Melachim* 11:3, 12:5.
4. *Sanhedrin* 91b, 99a; *Berachot* 34b; *Pesachim* 68a; *Shabbat* 63a. Cf. Maimonides, *Mishnah Torah, Hilchot Teshuvah* 9:2, and *Hilchot Melachim* 12:2.
5. *Tosafot, Rosh HaShanah* 16b, s.v. "*l'yom din*"; *Emunot V'Deot* 6:4; Ra'avad, *Hilchot Teshuvah* 8:8; *Kesef Mishnah, Teshuvah* 8:2; *Derech HaShem* 1:3:11.

6. Ramban, *Sha'ar HaGemul*, (translated by Rabbi Dr. Charles B. Chavel as *The Gate of Reward* [Shilo Publishing House, 1983]). According to the Ramban and other authorities, the World of Souls is also often referred to as the Garden of Eden.
7. *Sanhedrin* 99a.
8. Ramban, *Sha'ar HaGemul*. Citing Talmudic and Midrashic sources, the Ramban writes that there are three judgment days — three times the soul is judged: (1) Rosh HaShanah, the Jewish New Year, which reviews the past year and determines material circumstances for the upcoming year; (2) the day of death, when the decreased's life is reviewed (life review) and it is determined whether the soul needs to continue the trying experience of further review or is ready for paradise; and (3) the Great Day of Judgment, which is when all who lived are resurrected, the righteous for everlasting life (in a spiritualized physical world, according to the Ramban) and the wicked for what amounts to termination (according to others, there will be a middle category of those who are worthy to continue in a disembodied spirit form but not the more rarified physical form of the resurrected body in a resurrected world). There will also apparently be different degrees of reward (i.e., experiencing the Presence of God) in this renewed world after the Great Judgment Day, depending on one's life's actions.

   It has been asked, if a person is judged as to his status in the World to Come, what is the purpose of the Great Day of Judgment? One answer given is that after a person dies all the good and bad deeds and influences he had on others are "still in motion," and his children, too, when they do

good add to his merit. Only at the end of history can the "final tally" be made, then, as to the impact a person had on the world in his or her life (Rabbi Aharon Kotler, *Mishnat Aharon* I, p. 252).
9. *Derech HaShem* 1:3:13.
10. Ibid.
11. *Sha'ar HaGilgulim*, ch. 8; *Derech HaShem* 2:3:10.
12. Many are equally surprised to discover that reincarnation was an accepted belief by many of the great minds underpinning Western civilization. Plato, for instance (in *Meno, Phaedo, Timaeus, Phaedrus,* and *Republic*), espouses belief in the doctrine of reincarnation. He seems to have been influenced by earlier classic Greek minds, such as Pythagorus and Empedocles. In more modern times, Voltaire and Benjamin Franklin were among the thinkers of the eighteenth century, the Age of Enlightenment and Rationalism, who espoused the notion of reincarnation. In the nineteenth century, Schopenhauer wrote (*Parerga and Paralipomena*), "Were an Asiatic to ask me for a definition of Europe, I should be forced to answer him: It is that part of the world which is haunted by the incredible delusion that a person's present birth is his first entrance into life...." Dostoyevsky (in *The Brothers Karamazov*) refers to the idea, while Tolstoy seems to have been quite definite that he had lived before. Thoreau, Emerson, Walt Whitman, Mark Twain, and many others espoused some form of belief in reincarnation.

It should be noted, however, that some Jewish philosophers and commentators, especially tenth-century authority Rabbi Sa'adiah Gaon, denied reincarnation as a Jewish tenet (see *Emunot V'Deot* 6:3).

13. The Talmud relates that second-century sage Rabbi Shimon bar Yochai and his son Elazar fled to a cave to escape Roman persecution. For the next thirteen years they learned all day and night without distraction. According to kabbalistic tradition (*Tikunei Zohar* 1a), it was during those thirteen years that he and his son first composed the main teachings of the *Zohar*. Concealed for many centuries, the *Zohar* was published and disseminated by Rabbi Moshe de Leon in the thirteenth century.

14. *Zohar* I:186b.

15. Ibid. II:99b.

16. *Zohar* I:131a, I:186b, II:94a, II:97a, II:100a, II:105b, II:106a, III:88b, III:215a, III:216a; *Tikunei Zohar* 6 (22b, 23b), 21 (56a), 26 (72a), 31 (76b), 32 (76b), 40 (81a), 69 (100b, 103a, 111a, 114b, 115a, 116b), 70 (124b, 126a, 133a, 134a, 137b, 138b); *Zohar Chadash* 33c, 59a–c, 107a, Ruth 89a.

17. "Rabbi Yosei answered: 'Those bodies that were unworthy and did not achieve their purpose will be regarded as though they had not been.... Rabbi Yitzchak [disagreed and] said: For such bodies the Holy One will provide other spirits, and if found worthy they will be able to abide in the world, but if not, they will be ashes under the feet of the righteous" (*Zohar* I:131a; cf. *Zohar* II:105b).

18. The *Zohar* (III:216a) and *Tikunei Zohar* (6 [22b], 32 [76b]), for example, suggest three or four chances. The *Tikunei Zohar* (69 [103a]) suggests that if even a little progress is made each time, the soul is given even a thousand opportunities to come back in order to achieve its completion. The *Zohar* (III:216a) says that an essentially righteous person who experiences the travails of wandering from city to

city, from house to house — even to try to drum up business (*Zohar Chadash Tikunim* 107a) — is as if he undergoes many reincarnations.

19. The answer is yes, it's a possibility (*Zohar* II:106a).
20. "After the soul has left the body and the body remains without breath, it is forbidden to let it remain unburied (*Mo'ed Katan* 28a; *Bava Kama* 82b). For a dead body that is left unburied for twenty-four hours...prevents God's design from being fulfilled, for perhaps God decreed that he should undergo reincarnation at once on the day that he died, which would be better for him, but as long as the body is not buried, the soul cannot go into the presence of the Holy One nor be transferred into another body. For a soul cannot enter a second body until the first is buried..." (*Zohar* III:88b).
21. See *Tikunei Zohar* 70 (133a). Later kabbalists detail the circumstances that can lead to reincarnation in vegetative and even mineral form (*Sha'ar HaGilgulim*, ch. 22 and 29; *Sefer Chareidim* 33; *Ohr HaChaim* 1:26).
22. *Bahir* 195. *Bahir* 122, 155, 184, and 185 also discuss reincarnation.
23. In his commentary to Genesis 38:8 and Job 33:30.
24. For example, in his commentary to Genesis 34:1; see also his *Ta'amei HaMitzvos* 16a.
25. In his commentary to Genesis 4:25 and Deuteronomy 33:6.
26. His main works are *Eitz Chaim* (Tree of Life) and *Pri Eitz Chaim* (Fruit of the Tree of Life), as well as *Shemoneh She'arim* (Eight Gates), which deal with everything from Bible commentary to divine inspiration and reincarnation.
27. *Sefer HaGilgulim* (The Book of Reincarnations), by Rabbi

Chaim Vital, is also an entire book devoted to the topic.
28. In his commentary to *Niddah* 30b.
29. In his commentary to the book of Jonah and other places.
30. For example, Reb Meir Simchah of Dvinsk in his *Ohr Samei'ach (Hilchot Teshuvah* 5, s.v. "*v'yadati*"); the Chafetz Chaim, *Mishnah Berurah* 23:5 and *Sha'ar HaTzion* 702:6; Rabbi Yaakov Yisrael Kanievsky (the Steipler Gaon) in *Chayei Olam*.
31. Job 33:29.

Many Lives

> After all, it is no more surprising to be born twice than it is to be born once.
>
> *Voltaire*

Self-conscious best describes the experience many people have the first time they enter a bookstore to buy or browse through Dr. Brian Weiss's international bestseller, *Many Lives, Many Masters*. After all, most of us like to think of ourselves as essentially down-to-earth, well adjusted, and normal. However, in order to pick up a copy of *Many Lives* one will probably have to make an excursion down the Occult/New Age section — past books on UFOs, witchcraft, shamanism, tarot cards, black magic, and the like.

It does not matter that Dr. Weiss once headed the psychiatry wing of a major medical center, has been published in numerous psychiatric journals, has written for psychiatric textbooks, and generally knows more about psychology than the vast majority of the authors whose books are displayed in that section. It does not matter that his books deal with authentic psychotherapeutic case histories. It does not matter that respected therapists worldwide have used similar methods, albeit often clandestinely. It does not matter that Dr. Weiss himself was an intellectually well-equipped skeptic who only reluctantly came to his beliefs.

To the civilized Westerner, reincarnation is equated with the likes of crystal balls, black magic, star charts, snakehead elixirs, hokey personages of questionable character, and flippant movie stars. Simply put, it is a modern taboo. And *Many Lives* is a taboo challenger.

In 1980, a twenty-seven-year-old woman stepped into the Florida office of Dr. Brian L. Weiss. Catherine, as she is called in *Many Lives, Many Masters*, had numerous, deeply rooted phobias. Among them were fears of water, choking, the dark, flying, and death. Certainly not uncommon fears. Yet they were out of control and wreaking havoc in her life. She was so fearful that she would often sleep in a walk-in closet. Furthermore, she could not easily fall asleep at night, slept lightly when she did, and frequently experienced nightmares and sleepwalking episodes.

Dr. Weiss used conventional psychotherapy on Catherine for a year and a half, to no avail. Nothing seemed to work. Finally, she reluctantly agreed to allow him to use hypnotherapy.

Relaxed, in a deep trance, Catherine related long-forgotten memories of her childhood. In one, she recalled her terror at the age of six when a gas mask was placed over her face in a dentist's office. In another, at age five, she had been pushed into a swimming pool and nearly drowned. Yet another personal recollection — most significant of all — was the memory of Catherine's father abusing her when she was three. Usually, when suppressed traumatic memories such as these are unearthed, the patient experiences a release and the symptoms attached to each memory begin to alleviate. But the next week, when Catherine returned, her phobias were as pervasive as ever, including her fears of water and choking.

Dr. Weiss was bewildered. Something should have changed. Could it be, he thought, that an even earlier event happened that she was repressing? During the next session, Dr. Weiss quickly brought Catherine into a deep hypnotic trance and asked her the innocuous question "Go back to the time from which your symptoms arise." She began describing in vivid detail her life in an ancient time thousands of years before! In describing the end of a past life recalled during that session, she told how a flood or tidal wave was inundating her village and how the waters finally drowned her. Particularly traumatic was the lucid memory of the raging froth tearing her beloved infant from her arms.

Dr. Weiss did not know what to make of it. He believed it to be fantasy, though the clarity of her description was uncanny. Nevertheless, his years of training did not allow him to seriously consider the possibility that she was actually describing a past life.

Then a curious thing happened.

Catherine returned for her next session a week later and announced that her fear of water and drowning had vanished, her fear of choking was diminished, and she was sleeping much better. It was as if the incident of drowning in her past life was the repressed memory causing her present-day phobia!

Still, Dr. Weiss was very far from concluding that what she had described was real. After all, reincarnation!? How could it be? Even Catherine had trouble fully accepting it because it contradicted her religious beliefs.

Despite his skepticism, Dr. Weiss continued with this method of treatment. He hypnotized Catherine, who time and again described in detail numerous past lives. Catherine's symptoms continued to abate with each revelation of a parallel traumatic event in a past life.

Between sessions Dr. Weiss scoured scientific journals for precedence of such a case. Although the phenomenon was only minimally represented, some of the research was impressive, particularly that of Dr. Ian Stevenson (we will touch on some of Dr. Stevenson's research in the next chapter). Could it be that there really was such a thing as reincarnation and that it would explain Catherine's case? Dr. Weiss was not prepared to answer that question affirmatively. At least, not yet.

Then another curious thing happened.

Under hypnosis, Catherine began speaking in a husky voice, conveying some very uncharacteristically profound philosophical thoughts. Dr. Weiss was stunned. He would often bring Catherine to the day of death in a particular lifetime and ask her to tell him what she saw. Whether she died traumatically or peacefully, she invariably described the experience of death similar to that told by people who had near-death experiences. For instance, she would float above her body and be magnetically drawn toward an otherworldly light. Now, however, she claimed to be channeling information from an outside source! Later, during numerous other "in-between-life" states, she declared that the information was being conveyed to her by "master spirits."

The doctor did not know what to think. Catherine was not psychotic or on drugs. She was not an actress. She had no known motivation to create a hoax. And here she was speaking uncharacteristically esoteric thoughts in a very uncharacteristic tone, claiming to be a mouthpiece for "master spirits."

In the next session, a truly incredible and pivotal event took place. Following a past-life death experience, under deep hypnotic trance, Catherine, spontaneously and unprovoked, informed Dr. Weiss that his father and son were with her.

"Your father says you will know him because his name is Avraham.... His death was due to his heart. Your son's heart was also important, for it was backward, like a chicken's.... He [your son] made a great sacrifice for you out of his love. His soul is very advanced. His death satisfied his parents' debts. He wanted to show you that medicine could only go so far, that its scope is very limited."

Dr. Weiss was speechless. His father and son had indeed died, years before Catherine began therapy with him. His infant son, Adam, had died in the Northeast after only twenty-three days due to a very rare ailment where the veins of his heart were incorrectly routed, entering the heart on the wrong side as if it was backward. Modern medicine's inability to save his son's life convinced Dr. Weiss that "medicine could only go so far," just as Catherine had said and thus solidified his commitment to psychiatry. Perhaps most incredible, this Roman Catholic woman had told him his deceased father's Hebrew name (and not in its anglicized pronunciation, Abram or Abraham, but Avraham), even though those who knew him called him by his English name, Alvin, or his nickname, Reds!

Dr. Weiss was stunned. He could no longer deny the paranormal nature of Catherine's abilities. It was not a question of "Did it happen?" but rather a question of how to explain what happened. Rationalist explanations like fraud, cryptomnesia (sudden recall of a memory taken out of context), and genetic memory (memory somehow encoded in the genes one inherits from a parent) were all inadequate for these circumstances.

Telepathy? What did that show? To the rationally trained scientist with a mechanistic view of the human being, explanations like telepathy and spirit possession solved nothing. Reincarnation did not either, but Dr. Stevenson and others had documented some very impressive research suggesting the possibility. And once one got beyond the purely mechanistic view, it was as reasonable (or unreasonable) as anything else.

Catherine continued her therapy with Dr. Weiss for several months until she was cured. Normally a patient such as she has to be treated with medications, along with individual and group therapy, over many years. And even then the patient rarely gets cured. But when Catherine's last session ended, she had not only lost all her phobias, but she radiated a magnetism that automatically drew others to her. She was more than cured.

But Is It Science?

> [With] few exceptions...nearly everyone outside the range of orthodox Christianity...Islam, and science — the last being a secular religion for many persons — believes in reincarnation.
>
> *Dr. Ian Stevenson, Children Who Remember Past Lives*

Many Lives, Many Masters raised from the dead many questions regarding immortality and soul, submerged for the most part beneath nineteenth- and twentieth-century science, rationality, and skepticism. Dr. Weiss's firsthand experience caused people to think, "You mean, it could really be true?" One could even say that the twentieth-century mind secretly longed for a Dr. Weiss, a scientifically trained rationalist, to come along and legitimize its natural interest in such possibilities. And his book did that for many.

Many Lives is good reading. There is no question about

that. But is it science?[1] That's the first thought that crosses many a reader's mind. And it's a fair question.

Some people, like Dr. Weiss himself before treating Catherine, credit the experience to fantasy or wish fulfillment. The problem with that theory, Dr. Weiss claims, is that fantasy cannot produce the same kind of results. A therapist will not dramatically cure a patient with deep phobias by having him perform visualization exercises of a conjured up past life in some way related to that patient's crippling fears.

Another psychiatrist, Dr. Raymond Moody, a doubter of reincarnation, felt sure the phenomenon had to do with wish fulfillment. Then he allowed himself to be regressed. He thought that if he would experience anything his subconscious imagination would conjure up the lifetime of a Julius Caesar or some other famous historical personality. What he got were numerous very unceremonial lives. He had to admit that, whatever the experience was, it had nothing to do with wish fulfillment. Each of his past lives was less desirable than the previous one. And so it is with most patients. They experience the lives of average, not very famous personalities.[2]

Interestingly, though, not all therapists who use past-life therapy — and there are many of them worldwide — believe in reincarnation, even though they use the technique successfully in their practices. "I've said many times," Dr. Weiss admits, "that neither the therapist nor the patient have to believe in reincarnation for regression therapy to work. Patients will still come up with memories. The therapist, whether or not he or she believes it, will still be able to elicit these memories. And a clearing, a healing, will still occur."[3]

Nevertheless, Dr. Weiss asserts, "Personally, I do believe it." What does he say is the most impressive evidence for reincarnation? "Probably the cases of children reporting past lives. Dr. Ian Stevenson, professor and chairman emeritus of the Department of Psychiatry at the University of Virginia, has reported over two thousand cases of such children. And he is a very cautious and conservative researcher.

"It is very compelling," Dr. Weiss adds, "when children talk about 'the time when they were big' and then start coming out with details and facts. I myself have encountered children who claim to have lived past lives. One of them was a four-year-old boy who gave details about World War II bombers. How did he know this? Actually, he told me how: 'When I was big, I flew them,' he said."

Sometimes the consequences of such statements from children are frightening to ponder.

"A mother called me up," Dr. Weiss relates, "because her four-year-old daughter, previously healthy according to her, was about to be started on psychiatric medications for her delusion. What was her delusion? One day the mother came home with a bag of antique coins, one of which was six-sided. The daughter got very excited when she saw the coin and said, 'Look! Look! Mommy, don't you remember when I was big and you were a man — we had lots of those!'

"The daughter took that coin, slept with it, and would elaborate about her past in more detail. Her mother was frightened by this. Eventually they wound up with a child psychiatrist who recommended medication because the daughter's behavior persisted. When the woman contacted me, I took a case history and concluded that the daughter was normal. I told the mother that I thought it was a past-life memory fragment emerging, probably stimulated by the coin, and if she felt uncomfortable with her daughter's recollections, she should just say something like 'That's nice, dear, now let's get back to our finger painting.' She took that advice, and now the daughter is fine. I wonder how many other children have been mislabeled like that.

"Some of the stories are wonderful, fascinating, and hard to explain away," Dr. Weiss continues. "It wasn't my case, but a few years back parents of two-year-old twin boys noticed that the boys were speaking a rather sophisticated private language. They finally brought the twins to the Linguistics Department of Columbia University, where it was determined that the boys were speaking Aramaic to each other! Now, Aramaic is still spoken in a few remote villages in Syria, but basically it is extinct. And it is not the kind of language you hear on late-night television. As scientists and observers, as we all are, how do you explain that? Where is that coming from? You can't just say, 'No, it doesn't exist,' if it exists. You have to ask, how is the mind capable of speaking Aramaic at two and a half years old?"

This last phenomenon, where an ancient or foreign language is spoken by people who have had no prior exposure to it, is frequent enough to have its own name: xenoglossy (*xeno* meaning "strange" and *glossa* meaning "tongue"). Accounts of reincarnation supported by xenoglossy form a uniquely impressive type of evidence. Usually the more obscure the language that is recalled, the more convincing the claim that an actual past life has been accessed.[4]

Dr. Joel L. Whitton and Joe Fisher, authors of *Life Between Life*, record a case. A patient of Dr. Whitton's, who received therapy in his Canadian office, recalled two particularly convincing past lives under hypnosis. In one he was Thor, a Viking[5] leading a raiding party. In the other he was Xando, a Mesopotamian high priest.[6]

As Thor, he vividly recalled standing at the helm of his ship and yelling, "*Roko! Roko!*" which he took to mean, "Let's get out of here!" Dr. Whitton asked the patient to tell him other words he could hear himself saying as Thor. The patient was able to come up with twenty-two words, although they sounded like meaningless gibberish to his twentieth-century mind.

Dr. Whitton conferred with Icelandic and Norwegian linguistic experts. They told him that ten of the words were indeed Old Norse, the language of the Vikings. The word *roko* means "storm," which made sense because the patient described Thor as yelling that word when he first spotted a storm forming on the horizon. Several of the other words seemed to be derived from Russian, Serbian, and Slavic origin. Given that the Vikings were known to raid foreign lands, the presence of such non–Old Norse words only increased the case's authenticity. Almost all the words had something to do with the sea.

If that were not enough, Dr. Whitton asked the same patient for similar recollections of words he used as Xando. Instead of spoken words, this time the patient scribbled some Arabic-style lines and shapes on a pad. Again, he had no idea what he had done. The scribbles looked just like that: meaningless scribbles. Dr. Whitton showed the sample to Dr. Ibrahim Pourhadi, an expert in ancient Persian and Iranian languages at the Near Eastern section of Washington's Library of Congress. Dr. Pourhadi identified the scribbles as an authentic reproduction of a long dead Mesopotamian language.

This case is particularly impressive because the patient spoke or wrote down languages that are not used today and are known only to a few experts.[7] And yet, as impressive as cases such as these may be, virtually all agree that the work of Dr. Ian Stevenson possesses the most compelling evidence, at least from a purely scientific perspective.

Spanning both the Far East, where reincarnation is often an accepted belief, and the West, where it is usually not, Dr. Stevenson meticulously gathered information on some two thousand cases "suggestive of reincarnation," all involving children. His decision to focus on children is notable from a scientific standpoint because children are much less culturally indoctrinated than adults. When interviewed properly, they are less prone to express their experiences in ways that conform to cultural expectations. They are also more easily found out if they are making it up.

For a typical case, Dr. Stevenson would begin his research by traveling to India, or wherever the reported case might be, and conduct a thorough firsthand investigation by questioning all the parties involved, including the child. Then he would travel to the town where the child claimed to have lived, locate a family by the name given, and corroborate any or all of the other details.

Incredibly, more often than not Dr. Stevenson found that numerous details were accurate. Yet, even after he collected all the information and verified numerous claims, he did not stop there. He painstakingly analyzed the case point by point to see if any other possibility than reincarnation could be used to satisfactorily explain the information (such as fraud and contact between the two families). Some cases were stronger than others, and he noted those distinctions in his text.

To illustrate, one of his young subjects was Swarnlata Mishra.[8] When she was only three and a half years old, her father took her on a trip 170 miles from her home. Fifty-seven miles from their destination, she asked the driver of the truck to turn down a road to "my house." Over the next couple of years, Swarnlata gave other details of her previous life. Dr. Stevenson found out about the girl, conducted an interview, and collected forty-nine statements made by

Swarnlata related to her purported past life. Then he proceeded to corroborate them.

All but three were corroborated, including details of the colors and layout of the house in which she had supposedly lived in her past life (and which she had never seen in this life). Furthermore, she correctly identified relatives from the past life who were still alive and who were sitting commingled in a group of about forty others, and she correctly identified her son in the previous life despite the overt attempt of her other son in that lifetime to lie about who he was. As for the three details that were apparently incorrect, they had explanations.[9]

The strongest evidence, though, according to Dr. Stevenson, are cases involving what he refers to as "physical patterns."[10] Examples include deformities or birthmarks in the present life in the exact places where bullets or bladed weapons reportedly pierced the person in the previous life. Dr. Stevenson has collected more than two hundred such cases. For many of them, he has actually secured medical documents, such as hospital records or autopsy reports, that show that the individual in question was killed by a bullet or blade in a previous life in the place where the present-day birthmark is found.

A strong example of such a physical pattern is the case of Ravi Shankar.[11] At around the age of two, Ravi first asked his mother and older sister to supply him with the same toys he had when he was supposedly a person named Munna. It turns out that a six-year-old boy, Munna the son of Jageshwar, was brutally murdered several months before Ravi Shankar was born. He had been lured into an orchard by the murderers, who then slit his throat. The perpetrators were brought to trial and confessed to the murder, but then were released due to lack of witnesses. (Ravi reportedly passed them in the street one day, and though he had never been told who they were, he expressed extreme fear.)

When Ravi Shankar was thirteen, Dr. Stevenson conducted an interview with him that resulted in a list of twenty-six items he then subsequently sought to corroborate. All twenty-six were corroborated. Some were particularly noteworthy, like Ravi's description of a toy pistol that Munna loved. Most people in Munna's area were poor, and toys were considered a luxury. Yet Munna not only had toys but a favorite toy pistol, exactly as Ravi had related to Dr. Stevenson.

Yet, of all the particulars of this case, the most incredible was the congenital birthmark Ravi Shankar was born with. Dr. Stevenson writes:

> Under the ridge of the chin, some more to the right side than the left, I observed a linear mark crossing the neck in a traverse direction. It ran about two inches long and about one-eighth to one-quarter of an inch wide. It was darker in pigment than the surrounding tissue and had the stippled quality of a scar. It looked much like the healed scar of an old knife wound....[12]

Ravi Shankar was born with an unusual scar-like birthmark below his chin that was visible to the naked eye! (His parents said the birthmark had been longer and lower down across the neck when Ravi was born.)

Extrasensory perception or even spirit possession might explain at least a few aspects of some of Dr. Stevenson's other cases. But, Dr. Stevenson states, such explanations do not as satisfactorily explain the case of Ravi Shankar, which not only "requires some survivalist explanation" (i.e., that the spirit survives death) but "decisively favors reincarnation." And, as we said, Ravi Shankar is only one of more than two hundred such cases of birthmarks Dr. Stevenson has researched.

Does all this prove reincarnation?

It depends.

Dr. Weiss came to change his beliefs and accept reincarnation as a real fact of existence.

"I believe there is enough evidence to begin accepting this on the basis of data, not just belief," he asserts. "Although belief is extremely important," he adds.

He has dealt with some of the alternative explanations in his books,[13] including the possibility that regressed patients are merely tapping into a kind of Jungian collective unconscious. Although, he admits, some cases can be explained according to that, Jung's general archetypes do not account for cases where the patient recalls very specific knowledge never previously learned. For instance, they do not explain "people possessing detailed knowledge how to embalm bodies, how to make leather, how to churn butter, how to herd goats, how to fly World War II airplanes — to do all kinds of specific, detailed tasks that they have no knowledge of in their current lifetime."

Dr. Weiss states: "It is mostly the overwhelming cumulative weight of the clinical evidence that has convinced me. I alone have had now more than seven hundred individual patients, and many more in groups, who have gone through regression therapy and who have come up with things like names, dates, and details — a name in the Civil War, a name in World War II with a regiment.... The overwhelming number of people seen not just by me, but by many regression therapists around the world, as well as the variety of different people — attorneys, physicians, mechanics, plumbers — all coming up with the same type of information has convinced me."

He is not the only such person. Dr. Helen Wambach, author of *Life Before Life*, set out to disprove reincarnation. After hypnotizing hundreds of patients, however, she not only could not disprove it but became a staunch advocate herself.[14] (One of the things that helped convince her was how the accounts of those regressed to a past time proved to be historically accurate — even in the most subtle ways — over and over again.) And there are other people, including highly trained professionals, who now share a similar belief.

On the other hand, there are those who do not draw this conclusion. One such person is Dr. Raymond Moody, pioneer of contemporary near-death studies (see chapter 3 above, "Journey of the Soul") and author of his own book on reincarnation, *Coming Back: A Psychiatrist Explores Past-Life Journeys*. After a couple of years researching evidence for reincarnation, he remains noncommittal. He says he cannot definitely prove or disprove it.[15] To him, the most compelling evidence consists of "those puzzling few cases in which a past-life regression can be traced to an actual past life."[16] Nevertheless, science, he claims, has to dismiss them as "oddities" at this point. Despite that, and despite the fact that he himself is personally noncommittal, he writes that in his opinion if a trial were held to determine whether reincarnation is fact or fiction, the jury would conclude based upon the present evidence that it is fact.[17]

In Dr. Moody's discussion concerning proof for the existence of an afterlife, he makes an important distinction between proof and scientific proof.[18] On one hand, he states, "I don't think science can ever answer [the] question."[19] On the other hand, he admits answering affirmatively to those who ask him if near-death experiences are evidence of life after life. Furthermore, he reveals that after talking to "almost every NDE researcher in the world" most of them "believe in their hearts that NDEs are a glimpse of life after life."[20] Their failure to go public with a definitive statement is based on their inability (to date) to find a decisively conclusive proof in absolute scientific terms. Yet for the sake of their personal conviction the matter is apparently proven well enough.

Noteworthy, then, is the emphasis on scientific proof. Honest, responsible scientists admit that there is more to life than meets the scientific eye. Einstein wrote, "The most beautiful and most profound emotion we can experience is the sensation of the mystical.... Know that what is impenetrable to us really exists...."[21] Unfortunately, many do not share Einstein's depth of understanding. They are more likely to dismiss any ideas that might fall outside the box of science.

Science, for all its accomplishments, is nothing but a tool with its own limits. It, after all, was originally conceived by scientists and now must be studied by scientists. And scientists are human beings, prone to their own biases and expectations. Moreover, how can scientists attempt to shed scientific light on a subject that by definition is beyond the experience of the physical senses? Thus, to some people, no matter what evidence is presented, such research will always be an exercise in futility. They would say that if you are waiting for absolute proof of life after death or reincarnation you will have to wait forever (or at least until you pass on from this world — of course, by then it would be too late!).

If there is such a thing as scientific proof for reincarnation, it is in the work of Dr. Ian Stevenson. What is his conclusion? "A rational man can, if he wants, now believe in reincarnation on the basis of religious doctrine or cultural tradition."[22] Moreover, regarding his personal feelings on the matter, he states in his *Twenty Cases Suggestive of Reincarna-*

tion, "I argue that some of the cases do much more than suggest reincarnation; they seem to me to furnish considerable evidence for it."[23]

The question must be asked: If highly educated people such as Dr. Weiss and Dr. Stevenson, among others, are at least open to the possibility of reincarnation, why is *Many Lives, Many Masters* in the Occult/New Age aisle? Why is it not considered more mainstream? Why is it that when one expresses belief in reincarnation it elicits skeptical facial expressions or a noncommittal "That's nice. I'm happy for you"?

Dr. Weiss has pondered this question at great length. "When Catherine first began telling me of her past lives," he says, "I went to the libraries to see if anyone had reported similar cases. Other than the work of Dr. Stevenson, there was virtually nothing on the subject. Yet I couldn't believe I was the only one who had ever encountered such a case. I alone now have done regression work with so many people individually and in groups that it is clear to me that this phenomenon is quite common. What keeps people from reporting those cases? What keeps us from studying this more? I thought a lot about questions like that and concluded it was nothing but close-mindedness. And soon I began to understand why.

"Fear.

"Psychiatrists, psychotherapists, psychologists, social workers, nurse clinicians, are people. Everyone is afraid of the same thing — of being considered weird or strange or different, of peer approval or disapproval — and so they don't write about their unconventional thoughts and experiences, even though they may not be so rare. Even within families, I have often found that one person with vivid and wonderful experiences hasn't even told the others in the family. They are afraid of the same disapproval.

"It is so important to not be afraid, to start sharing these experiences, because it helps in healing grief, in understanding life, in gaining values and perspective. In the beginning, I was very afraid, too. Even after Catherine had been cured, it took four years to write *Many Lives*. I was afraid of professional reaction. I was running a department in a conservative hospital. But more and more patients came in with past-life memories. And then professionals of all types started entrusting me with their experiences — and it just seemed too important to not write the book.... Now one of the things I do is encourage people to keep an open mind."

This could explain why professionals concerned with their reputations might react with such strong denial. But it does not really explain the skepticism one encounters outside the office, from the everyday person in the street. For them, Dr. Weiss suggests an additional reason.

"I think that people in Westernized countries are simply not aware of the role reincarnation plays in their own religions, whether Christianity or Judaism. We are a secularized society, and most of us are just not knowledgeable in this area."

His point is well taken. He himself has encountered many Jews, for instance, who are surprised to hear that their religion contains belief in reincarnation. Apparently it's an easy mistake to make, as evidenced by the fact that more than one "expert" has written that Orthodox Judaism denies the concept of reincarnation.[24] The truth is, however, that the idea of *gilgul*, or reincarnation, is a very ancient Jewish tradition and has been more or less widely accepted among the Jewish masses since the late sixteenth century. As Dr. Weiss points out, though, their wonder has to do with the fact that contemporary Jews are not particularly well acquainted with their traditions, and even less so with their religion's esoteric traditions.

A similar phenomenon exists among Christians, although for different reasons. References to reincarnation in the writings of the early Christians were later declared heretical and officially banned from Church doctrine in the Council of Nice in the year 553. The idea resurfaced periodically over the ensuing centuries within the context of various mystically inclined movements. However, those Christians, along with their ideas, were often systematically, and sometimes brutally, stamped out. Thus, whether stems from general ignorance or planned suppression, the result is the same for the average Westerner: reincarnation is a foreign idea.

And yet ignorance does not seem to explain it all. The very thought of reincarnation seems to touch a cultural sore spot.

Taboo has several definitions in the dictionary. It is defined as a prohibition extending from "a fear of immediate harm from mysterious superhuman forces." This definition conjures up images of ancient idol-worshiping cultures centered around obedience to the various deities. Another definition, more applicable to our modern situation, pinpoints it as a "prohibition imposed by social custom." It is something "banned as constituting a risk." These definitions of *taboo* get to the crux of the matter.

There are social norms, beyond even those of the professional world, that play an enormous role in defining who we are. A baby born in the United States seventy-five years ago would more than likely grow up to be an ardent capitalist. Chances are, though, that the same baby born at the same time, but in China, would have grown up waving a little red flag and yelling, "Mao! Mao!" at communist rallies. We are very much creatures of our environment.

On the other hand, it is true that we possess enormous individuality — at least in potential.[25] Though social standards can overpower the individual — and history is replete with many famous and many, many more not so famous examples — a person can always overcome social gravity. Nevertheless, how many really ever develop the herculean thrust necessary to catapult themselves into regions beyond the downward pull of social norms? Whether it is fear of the imaginary — the "mysterious forces" rampant in ancient idolatrous cultures — or the fear of image ("What will people think?"), our societal taboos play an enormous role in who we are (or, perhaps better put, in who we are prevented from becoming). In this light, the words told to Dr. Weiss by Catherine under deep hypnotic trance are insightful:

> You [Dr. Weiss] must eradicate the fears from their minds. It is a waste of energy when fear is present. It stifles them from fulfilling what they were sent here to fulfill.... They must first be put into a level very, very deep.... It's only on the surface...that the trouble lies. Deep within their soul, where the ideas are created, that is where you must reach them.... Energy...everything is energy. So much is wasted.... Inside the mountain it is quiet; it is calm at the center. But on the outside is where the trouble lies. Humans can only see the outside, but you can go much deeper. You have to see the volcano. To do it you have to go deep inside.... This energy must not be wasted. You must get rid of the fear....[26]

Those parts of ourselves deep within, the bubbling fires inside the "volcano" — those impenetrable recesses of our souls — are what we long for most. It is the part that knows what we were "sent here to fulfill." But fear blocks us. Cultural taboos have "banned [it] as constituting a risk."

Is reincarnation such a taboo? Is it a forgotten doorway leading to matters that at some level threaten the status quo of normative society?

Perhaps.

Or perhaps, some people will contend, it is entirely different. The fear is nothing more than a natural reflex to a repulsive concept, a concept originating in primitive society's need for ready-made answers to the question of mortality and life's injustices.

However one wishes to view it, there is no doubt that the possibilities and implications of reincarnation have the power to touch our primal human emotions.

Notes

1. In some ways, it is more scientific than the controlled, anecdotal investigations by Dr. Stevenson. After all, Dr. Weiss was not looking for evidence for the existence of reincarnation. In fact, he patently denied it, even after he began curing Catherine using past-life therapy. Moreover, it would be hard to seriously accuse him of ulterior motives given that he jeopardized a prestigious career with the publication of *Many Lives*. These considerations alone convey an air of authenticity that classic laboratory science cannot easily match. Nevertheless, this chapter, "But Is It Science?" will explore whether scientific inquiry in the most broadly understood sense of the term can verify the possibility of reincarnation.
2. *Coming Back: A Psychiatrist Explores Past-Life Journeys* (co-authored with Paul Perry), pp. 25–26.
3. Unless otherwise noted, all the quotes from Dr. Weiss in this chapter are from interviews or correspondence with Dr. Weiss.

4. Dr. Ian Stevenson has published an entire book on the subject: *Xenoglossy: A Review and Report of a Case.*
5. *Life Between Life*, pp. 167–68.
6. Ibid., p. 169.
7. This would constitute an example of what the psychical researchers call "xenoglossy," where the subject can only *recite* words and phrases of a foreign language, but cannot converse in that language. By comparison, "responsive xenoglossy" is when the subject freely converses in a language not learned through normal channels. For instance, one of Dr. Stevenson's more meticulously researched cases involves an American woman who conversed in Swedish during hypnotic sessions without having learned it previously! That is an example of responsive xenoglossy, and, according to the researchers, such a case would present even more impressive evidence than recitive xenoglossy.
8. *Twenty Cases Suggestive of Reincarnation*, pp. 63–79.
9. For instance, though Swarnlata incorrectly said that one of her names had been Kamlesh (in addition to the correct and only name she had been called by, Biya), later investigation revealed that Swarnlata had indeed apparently been a person named Kamlesh, but in a second, altogether different previous life than the one mentioned above.
10. *Twenty Cases Suggestive of Reincarnation*, pp. 34–50, 206–19, 222–40, 348–49. Dr. Stevenson has dedicated an entire book on the subject: *Where Reincarnation and Biology Intersect*. It is a much shorter version of his multivolume *Reincarnation and Biology: A Contribution to the Etiology of Birthmarks and Birth Defects*, which reflects thirty years of research.
11. *Twenty Cases Suggestive of Reincarnation*, pp. 79–93.

12. Ibid., p. 90.
13. Besides *Many Lives, Many Masters*, Dr. Weiss has written *Through Time into Reality, Only Love Is Real: A Story of Soulmates Reunited*, and *Messages from the Masters: Tapping into the Power of Love*.
14. Initially motivated by a desire to debunk reincarnation, Dr. Wambach conducted a ten-year survey, beginning in the late 1960s, of the past-life recalls under hypnosis of 1,088 subjects. She asked very specific questions about the time periods in which people lived and the clothing, footwear, utensils, money, housing, etc., that they used or came in contact with. Wambach found people's recollections to be amazingly accurate. With the exception of eleven subjects, all descriptions of clothing, footwear, and utensils were consistent with historical records.
15. One of the arguments Dr. Moody cites questioning the scientific validity of reincarnation is the fact that the evidence for it is not reproducible. "Reproducible evidence in the case of reincarnation and science," he writes, "would be the ability to prove that, say, white rats recently born had indeed lived before in the same laboratory."

    Taken from another angle, though, the similar experiences between people of ancient cultures (as recorded, for instance, in the chronicles of ancient Egypt and Tibet) and modern-day people indicates that the phenomenon is reproducible over time — extremely long periods of time — as well as across cultures. Is this type of reproducibility scientific? Not if one thinks of science exclusively in terms of lab rats.

    On the other hand, to some the above would consti-

But Is It Science? 133

tute an acceptable form of scientific evidence. In fact, Dr. Moody himself used the same argument in *Life After Life* (p. 238) to help support the authenticity of near-death experiences. He wrote: "The similarities and parallels among the writings of ancient thinkers and the reports of modern Americans who survive close brushes with death" lend support to the authenticity of near-death experiences.

Thus, if one wants to confine oneself to lab rats, one does not have reproducibility. If one wants to define the term in a broader sense, one can find reproducibility. The choice of which argument sounds better to an individual probably extends as much from some motivation buried deep within that individual's psyche as from anywhere else. (By the way, Dr. Moody admits to a bias [in *Coming Back*, p. 103], namely, that he is "a scientist influenced by a Christian rearing," and that upbringing, he admits, has played a part in his evaluation of the evidence for reincarnation.)

16. *Coming Back*, p. 187; cf. pp. 107–15. Dr. Moody himself relates several examples of such cases in his book (*Coming Back*, pp. 108–15). One man under hypnosis remembered his name, place of birth, and the time period in which he had lived previously. The man then researched the information and obtained records that showed that a French nobleman named Antoine Poirot, as he had remembered himself, had been born in the time and place he had recalled under hypnotic regression.

Another person, a woman, relived the traumatic experience of being trapped in the hollow of a snow mound with survivors of a group of American pioneers who stayed alive by resorting to cannibalism. Although the woman had no conscious memory of ever having learned about it (she was a recent immigrant to America and had never learned U.S. history), she described in detail an incident known as the Donner tragedy of 1846.

Dr. Moody also reports the case of an Indian artist who recalled his life as a minor French composer. Under hypnosis, the patient began speaking in a heavy French accent, although he had never learned French. He also described Paris vividly. Later research found this minor composer to have been a real person.

17. *Coming Back*, p. 190.
18. *The Light Beyond*, p. 197.
19. Ibid., p. 194.
20. Ibid., p. 193.
21. From his essay, "The World as I See It," originally published in *Forum and Century* 84: 193–94, the thirteenth in the *Forum* series, Living Philosophies. It is also included in *Living Philosophies* (New York: Simon Schuster, 1931), pp. 3–7.
22. Cited in "Reincarnation: A Doctor Looks Beyond Death," by Alton Slagle, *New York Sunday News* (August 4, 1974).
23. P. 2. It should be noted that Stevenson has his critics. Paul Edwards, in *Reincarnation: A Critical Examination*, cites many of them who, like him, believe Stevenson's work is fatally flawed, including accusations of asking leading questions, conducting superficial investigations, taking insufficient account of the "human fallibility" of the witnesses he interviews, and reporting the cases in a way that makes them sound more impressive than they are.

Of course, some of Edwards's accusations are themselves open to accusation. For instance, he makes the assumption (p. 255) "If Stevenson's reports are evidence for reincarnation, they must also be evidence for the collateral assumptions [like claims that reincarnating souls originated not from a previous life on this earth but another planet]." However, as we saw with the NDE research, a valid core experience is not necessarily immune from embellishment by the person experiencing it. Therefore, just because a case suggesting reincarnation includes a person who says he came from another life on a different planet does not necessarily invalidate the entire case and certainly not every other case suggesting reincarnation. The point is that Edwards's assumption that "collateral assumptions" must be accepted along with the core experience is flawed reasoning.

Edwards also admits that not everyone agrees Stevenson's methods are flawed, as he says (p. 255) when he cites the editor of the prestigious *Journal of Nervous and Mental Disease*, Dr. Eugene Brody, "who appears not to see any significant flaws in Stevenson's investigative procedures."

The bottom line is that, at the very least, in trying to make Stevenson's suppositions seem absurd, even Edwards acknowledges that if these cases are not the product of lies and fallible observations, they would constitute legitimate evidence for reincarnation, even if we can't explain how reincarnation works.

One final note: In the revised edition of *Children Who Remember Past Lives* (2001), Dr. Stevenson addresses and critiques many of the criticisms leveled against his work.

24. For instance, the authors of the book *Life Between Life* (pp.

61–62) dogmatically assert that Orthodox Judaism denies the principle. It's hard to pinpoint the source of their confusion other than the fact that they are not knowledgeable of the primary sources. All Jewish mystics, without exception, were what one would today call Orthodox Jews, and they took the belief in reincarnation as a given, as evidenced in their writings.

25. The biblical paradigm of such individuality is Abraham. God told him, "Go get yourself away from your country, your birthplace, your father's house..." (Genesis 12:1). Three levels of social forces are enumerated: "your country" — the nationalistic, political ideology; "your birthplace" — the more local, socialistic undertows; "your father's house" — even the particular familial expectations and norms. Abraham's future success began when he first broke away from those environmental forces. And, as Jewish mystics comment, the words "Go get yourself away" in Hebrew can be read as "Go *to* yourself." Only by breaking away from the external forces that operate upon our selves can we hope to find our true selves, our destiny.

26. *Many Lives, Many Masters*, p. 121.

Past Lives, Past Debts, Living Lessons

> The body of B. Franklin, printer, like the covers of an old book, its contents torn out and stripped of its lettering and gilding, lies here, food for worms. But the work shall not be lost, for it will, as he believed, appear once more in a new and more elegant edition, revised and corrected by the author.
>
> *Benjamin Franklin*

Judaism emphasizes that our hardships are not pointless. They are custom-designed to help us achieve our ultimate destiny.[1] This, of course, is very reassuring. Believing that all of one's struggles are meaningless is one of the greatest causes of emotional pain.

The classic example is the archetypal sufferer, Job. After an involved attempt by his friends to help him deal with his horrific suffering, he is consoled only when he becomes convinced that the Creator has some reason for giving him the afflictions (even though he does not even learn what those reasons are).

The lesson of Job is universal. Nothing is more demoralizing and unhealthy than the belief that one bears a heavy burden in vain. Conversely, there is no greater comfort than knowing that our suffering is not pointless.

A perspective purporting to suggest that life's hardships are not random — that they are somehow part of a higher design — clashes with everything modern morality and science have come to supposedly enlighten us with. Many modern scientists and thinkers believe life's happenstances are random; they are no less purposely designed than the random bang that gave birth to the universe. To say there is an underlying order and reason to the world's chaos and suffering is wishful thinking, according to them. The problem is that more and more people educated in this society are finding such a stance less and less tenable.

There is a story told by a rabbi in Jerusalem who delivered a class to doctors entitled "Ethics and Medicine."[2] A nonreligious doctor attending the lecture approached him after class and presented the rabbi the following dilemma.

"There was a lonely old man on the ward who was being kept alive on a respirator. He was a human vegetable, and there was no family to look after him. Since there was nobody to pull the plug, I had mercy and pulled the plug myself," the doctor admitted. "I didn't think much of it. In fact, I thought I was doing a good thing. But that night I had a dream. The deceased man came to me and said, 'I am summoning you to the court On High. You took away eleven days of my life. In those eleven days I would have been cleansed of my earthly blemishes. Now, however, because you deprived me of my suffering down there, I am incomplete and suffering up here.'

"Naturally I ignored the dream," the doctor told the rabbi, "but the next night the same dream recurred. I ignored it again, but it recurred a third time, last night. Now I am afraid that it is more than a dream. I think the deceased man is really communicating with me. I need your advice, Rabbi. What do you think I should do?"

"Since Jewish law," the rabbi told him, "views pulling the plug as an act of murder, even if you allow yourself to feel sincere remorse, you will at best only remove the blemish from your soul. Such remorse, however, cannot remove the negative effect on the person who had been deprived of eleven days of his life. Therefore, I recommended that you publicize the story in the hope that as a result people will come to appreciate the gift of life more. The merit of that should stand for the deceased man to relieve his suffering."

If this way of looking at the world sounds strange to modern ears, Dr. Weiss would be the first to concur. His life experiences, however, have taught him otherwise. In fact, it was the death of his twenty-three-day-old infant that started him on this odyssey culminating in *Many Lives, Many Masters*.

"He [the infant son who died] made a great sacrifice for you out of his love," Dr. Weiss was told by Catherine while she was under hypnosis. "His death satisfied his parents' debts." The exact nature of the debts incurred was never made clear to him. However, he has no doubt that they existed.

"We have debts that must be paid," Catherine uttered another time. "If we have not paid out these debts, then we must take them into another life.... You progress by paying your debts. Some souls progress faster than others.... If something interrupts your ability to pay a debt, you must return to the plane of recollection, and there you must wait until the soul you owe the debt to has come to see you. And when you both can be returned to the physical form at the same time, then you are allowed to return."[3]

In other words, one way to pay back such debts as the one the doctor incurred by depriving his patient of eleven days of his life is through reincarnation. Perhaps in the next life he would be given a child who lives only eleven days, and in this way the patient would get a chance to live out those eleven days he lost. And the death of the child would cause the doctor to suffer the anguish he should have felt when he deprived his patient of those eleven days. One might look at this death as an injustice — why should the father have to suffer so? Why should a child live such a short life? But it would all be explained if one knew that there is a purpose behind it all, that this happened due to past debts.

Past Lives, Past Debts, Living Lessons 141

The complex machinations involved in intertwining souls from previous lives into the fabric of a present life in order to orchestrate the payback of a past debt are mind-boggling. Those machinations are compounded when we consider the possibility that debts and paybacks may involve not just life-and-death issues, but even literal monetary debts as well.

The story is told about the Ba'al Shem Tov, the founder of the chassidic movement (some 250 years ago).[4] One day he asked his disciple and eventual successor, the Maggid of Mezeritch, to travel to a forest, climb a particular tree near a spring of water, wait till sundown, and then go home.

The Maggid of Mezeritch did so unhesitatingly, even though he did not know what his mentor intended. He climbed the tree and waited. After a while, a soldier appeared on horseback. He dismounted, ate, drank from the spring, and lay down for a nap. Eventually he rode off, not noticing that his purse of gold coins had fallen from the horse. Shortly thereafter a boy came along. He saw the purse, picked it up, and continued on his way.

The Maggid of Mezeritch watched from his hiding place in the tree as a tired-looking old man dressed in rags approached the spring next. He ate a crust of bread, drank a little water, and fell asleep. Just then the soldier returned, shook the old man awake, and demanded his purse of gold coins. The old man did not know what the soldier was talking about and denied having seen the purse. The soldier did not believe him and beat him mercilessly. Eventually he rode off in anger. When the Maggid of Mezeritch returned home, he asked his mentor, the Ba'al Shem Tov, for an explanation of what he had witnessed.

"In a previous incarnation, the soldier owed a debt to the boy for exactly the amount of money in the purse," he answered.

"I see," responded the Maggid of Mezeritch. "But why was the old man beaten up?"

"He had been the judge in the previous life who unjustly handed down the decision awarding the money to the wrong person. Now he has received his *tikun* (rectification)."

Ultimately reincarnation suggests that suffering is not pointless. Suffering is soil of the soul. Just as soil effects a breakdown and decay in objects in order to bring about an eventual blossoming, so each hardship we overcome, each lesson we learn, produces the equivalent of a new, beautiful petal or a deeper shade of color or a sturdier stem in our souls.

We see this principle in our everyday lives. We hear stories about people who achieve something in life by rising from the devastation of a dark and hopeless situation. People who overcame bereavement or holocaust; people who overcame addiction or disease; people who overcame poverty, illiteracy, or prejudice; people who were abused, abandoned, or neglected — these stories fill our papers because they give us hope and remind us that we, too, can turn our bleakest circumstances into areas of triumph. Reincarnation entails extending that principle to include the greater person, the person whose being encompasses more than the seventy or eighty years he may exist in this life.

It's not always necessary to fall back on reincarnation to explain suffering, yet it is an internally logical and authentic approach to the question. This is not to say that the average person can necessarily work out all the details in his or her given situation, but the mere recognition that reincarnation exists as a vehicle for divine justice contains the seed that answers life's most difficult questions.[5]

It should be clear by now that reincarnation, as a vehicle of divine justice, is not a simple matter. Practically speaking, the complex details necessary to understand how it applies in a given situation may leave many with more questions. Nevertheless, in general it is a logical approach to understanding the sticky issue of hardship and suffering. Our problems are not random. They do not always have to be due to a past-life debt, but sometimes they can be.

Beyond suffering and the issue of past debts, there are other dimensions to the topic of reincarnation. A past life may have a decisive impact on one's character.

"We will all have a dominant trait," Catherine related to Dr. Weiss. "This might be greed.... Then you must overcome this in that lifetime. You must learn to overcome greed. If you do not, when you return, you will have to carry that trait, as well as another one, into your next lifetime. The burdens will become greater. With each life that you go through and you did not fulfill these debts, the next one will be harder.... You are responsible for the life you have."[6]

Unbeknownst to Catherine and Dr. Weiss, a similar sentiment was expressed two centuries earlier by the great genius of Vilna, the Vilna Gaon:

> The main thing [to keep in mind is that the purpose of reincarnation] is to effect the repair of a [negative] influence originating in a previous lifetime.... [One way] to discern exactly what that negative influence is, is to reflect upon the type of wrong your soul yearns for most in this lifetime. That which you yearn for most is likely something you became habituated to in a previous life. Therefore, pay attention to your vices [for they tell you exactly what you have to work on in this lifetime].[7]

In *Many Lives*, Catherine tells Dr. Weiss several examples concerning a negative character trait she had to overcome in this life because of something that had happened in her past life.

> [In a previous life] I learned about hate, misdirected hate...people who hate and they don't know why. We are driven to it...by the evil when we are in a physical state.... I learned about [the futility of] anger and resentment, about harboring your feelings toward people. I also had to learn that I have no control over my life. I want control, but I don't have any.... We must have faith....[8]

Catherine also states that people of the "religious orders" have come closer to the true path because they have taken certain "vows," that is, they have committed themselves wholeheartedly. "The rest of us," she says, "continue to ask for rewards — rewards and justifications for our behavior.... The reward is in doing, but doing without expecting anything."[9]

Overcoming hatred, having faith, not asking for rewards — these are areas of personal development with great practical relevance in our daily lives. Overcoming hatred or resentment, for instance, is an important skill in successful negotiation, be it in a business or family setting. Having faith in oneself — or faith that if one is patient circumstances will conspire to work out for the best — is the cornerstone of personal power. Not asking for rewards can be reformulated to mean focusing on the process rather than the result, which is a formula for success applicable in all fields of endeavor.

What is profound here is that these personal development ideas tie into much more than our business or even personal lives; they also relate to lives we may have lived long ago. It suggests that we are much more than our isolated ego as it has manifested itself in this world over the past few decades.

Another area where reincarnation is a factor is in the concept of soulmates.

> And with the rib, which God had taken from man, he made a woman, and brought her to the man.

> And Adam said, "This time, bone of my bone, flesh of my flesh."[10]

How did Adam recognize in an instant that this creature was bone of his bone, flesh of his flesh? How did he know that she was his counterpart? He must have been created with some inborn sense of self, some preexistent image of this feminine counterpart implanted in his soul.

Indeed, the Talmud describes the experience of "soulmates" as a heavenly echo:

> Forty days before the creation of a child, an echo issues forth from heaven, proclaiming, "The daughter of So-and-so is destined for So-and-so...."[11]

At the moment of conception, an echo rings out, declaring So-and-so is destined for So-and-so. This echo may emanate from a mysterious abode above time and space, it may have to twist and meander its way through untold dimensions, but at some point it will resonate in two human hearts and often register with a meeting of eyes, like Adam opening his eyes and seeing Eve for the first time.

The Ari expanded this thought to include the possibility that the recognition emanates not only from a preexistent image but from an actual prior life.

> There are many reasons a soul might reincarnate. First, it may be because a person transgressed the Torah and returns to rectify that transgression. Second, it may be to complete an act he previously

> failed to perform. Yet a third reason is for the sake of others, to guide and rectify them.... There are other reasons as well, such as in order to marry his soulmate [*zivug rishon*], having not merited to do so the first time.[12]

Sometimes, the Talmud states, the soulmates identified by the heavenly echo do not marry, because they did not merit it. They may have met but missed the opportunity due to immaturity or some other factor that stunted their spiritual development. Perhaps their lack of readiness led divine providence to have them avoid meeting at all. In such a case, the Talmud goes on to explain, divine providence arranges for them to marry other mates. This is called a *zivug sheini*, literally, "second marriage."

> Sometimes a person will not merit his soulmate the first time, and a wife is arranged for him according to his deeds. From the souls of all the women of the world, there are none as close to him as this woman even though she is not his actual soulmate. When he needs to reincarnate, he will do so with this wife, even though she is not his actual soulmate.[13]

In other words, even a "non-echo" marriage is made in heaven and purposeful, if not as fulfilling. Everything comes down to free will. If two true soulmates do not work on themselves, they may never marry, and even if they do marry, they may end up living very unhappily ever after. Conversely, if two "non-echo" soulmates work on themselves and their marriage, they can reap all the joys and benefits of their labor.

Nevertheless, according to the Ari, the original soulmates are destined to be together to work through and accomplish what they were destined to accomplish, whether in this life or another:

> Sometimes he may have already married his soulmate, but transgressed in some way and must return to rectify it....[14]

They eventually come back and undergo all the trials and tribulations of life before meeting each other as if for the first time. If they merit it, they will have the opportunity to rectify the mistakes and shortcomings of the previous life together. This, according to the Ari, is what the Talmud really means by the term *zivug sheini*, a "second marriage." It does not necessarily mean a person's second marriage in this life, or even a "non-echo" marriage, but a true soulmate couple's first marriage in a second life together.[15]

Dr. Weiss's book, *Only Love Is Real*, is a "story of soulmates reunited." Even though there are innumerable other accounts and books of people claiming to have lived past lives together, and though Dr. Weiss himself has worked with couples who recalled past lives together under hypnosis, never before had he encountered such a strong case.

Elizabeth and Pedro, as Dr. Weiss calls them, had never met and didn't know the other existed even though they were each in therapy with him over a period of several

Past Lives, Past Debts, Living Lessons 149

months. Neither did they have any idea the memories they were recalling described identical lifetimes from different perspectives. Even Dr. Weiss did not recognize the similarities. The key lifetime they shared occurred in Jerusalem some two thousand years ago.

Under hypnosis, Elizabeth, who is not Jewish, "remembered the stones of Jerusalem with their distinctive coloring, which would change according to the light of the day and night. At times golden, at other times a tinge of pink or beige. But the golden color would always return. She remembered her town near Jerusalem with the small dirt and rock roads, the houses, the inhabitants, their clothing, their customs. There were some vineyards and some fig trees, some fields where flax and wheat grew. Water came from the well down the road...."

Her father, whose name was Eli in that life, worked as a potter. Elizabeth, who remembered she was a young girl named Miriam, described in detail her father's warmth, gentle touch, and sense of humor. She loved her father dearly. Then one day a couple of Roman soldiers arrived in the village and brutalized him for sport, tying his ankles to a horse and dragging him over some rocks. When they were finished with him, he was coughing up blood and dying. Little Miriam ran to him, cradled his head in her lap, and told him she loved him as she watched the life leave his eyes. She never recovered from the tragedy. She became deeply depressed and died young in that life.

Several weeks later Pedro went into a deep trance in

Dr. Weiss's office and recounted the life of a man who was dragged over some rocks by soldiers dressed in short leather uniforms and boots. As he lay there dying, his daughter ran over to him, wailing and sobbing, cradling his head in her lap. "I love you, Father," he heard her say softly as the pain disappeared, and he found himself looking down at his crumpled body, his head and shoulders resting limply in his daughter's lap.

The story evoked the emotion-laden memory of Dr. Weiss's son's tragic death. That, along with his heavy schedule and the time that had elapsed since Elizabeth's recounting of the same incident, prevented him from connecting the two stories at the time.

In the ensuing weeks, both Elizabeth and Pedro continued their therapy, neither aware that the other even existed. Anxiety caused by their personal issues had diminished under the doctor's guidance. One day, under hypnotic trance, Pedro again recounted to Dr. Weiss the life of the man dragged to his death by leather-clad soldiers. Assuming there was more his patient needed to learn from that experience, Dr. Weiss tried to draw out more details and asked Pedro if he knew his name in that life.

He pondered and finally answered, "No."

Suddenly a name popped into Dr. Weiss's mind. "Eli," he said. "Is your name Eli?"

"How do you know that?" Pedro asked, shocked. "That is my name. Some call me Elihu, and some call me Eli.... How do you know?"

Past Lives, Past Debts, Living Lessons 151

Dr. Weiss did not know why that name popped into his head. He had not yet put two and two together. "I don't know," he told his amazed patient.

Later that evening, the puzzle pieces fell into place, and he made the connection. He recalled that two months earlier Elizabeth had recounted the life of the daughter while Pedro had recounted the life of the father. It was one and the same lifetime from two perspectives!

Just as remarkably, he reviewed his notes and realized that other lives the two had told him about in the privacy of his office were likewise the same lifetimes retold by two people from different perspectives. In those lifetimes they had been childhood friends unable to marry, as well as husband and wife whose lives were destroyed by marauding barbarians.

The evidence was clear. Elizabeth and Pedro were two souls who had a long history together, even though they had no idea the other existed in this life.

Constrained by the laws of psychiatry and confidentiality, Dr. Weiss felt he could not tell them about each other. Yet he felt that if he had been put in the position to bring these two together, what right did he have to hold back the information?

In the end, he decided to "nudge destiny along" and arranged to have their appointments come out one after the other. There was also a time factor involved, since both patients were planning to leave the area for opposite parts of the continent in a few weeks.

Despite Dr. Weiss's efforts, destiny seemed not to favor the two soulmates getting together in this life. When they passed each other in the waiting room, they were cordial, but nothing more came of it. Dr. Weiss tried the same tactic again, but then, too, nothing more came of it. Finally, the weeks passed, and Pedro and Elizabeth each ended their therapy with Dr. Weiss.

However, destiny was not to be denied.

The day Pedro boarded a plane to New York, Elizabeth had tickets for a flight to Boston. Arriving at the airport, she was disappointed to find out her flight had been canceled. When they offered her an alternate flight to Newark, New Jersey, from which she could find a way to Boston for her business meeting, she took it. It was the same flight Pedro was scheduled to fly on.

Before either of them boarded the flight, Pedro sat in the waiting lounge and noticed a woman out of the corner of his eye. He realized she was the woman he had seen in Dr. Weiss's office. At the same moment, Elizabeth became aware that a strange man was staring at her. She felt very uncomfortable, frowned at him, then smiled when she recognized him from the office. He approached her and began a conversation. They decided to take seats next to each on the flight, and their relationship, like the plane, took off. They eventually married, had a child, and told Dr. Weiss that they were truly happy together.

Is this account scientific proof that reincarnation and soulmates exist? Is it anything more than interesting anecdotal evidence? Though this story did not take place in the sterile, controlled atmosphere of a laboratory, it is important to note some of the outstanding features of this account.

Ideally experiments in the social sciences need to be double-blind, meaning that neither the subjects of the experiment nor the ones conducting the experiment know important details about what is being done (or, better yet, that anything is being done at all).

The Pedro and Elizabeth account was double-blind, because even the one administering the experiment, so to speak — Dr. Weiss himself — had no idea there was an "experiment" going on. In fact, even when Pedro first recounted his life and death as Eli, Dr. Weiss did not connect it to the story he heard from Elizabeth weeks before. Then, when he did make the connection, not only were there descriptions of parallel past lives of father and daughter but of a life where they were friends who did not get to marry and then husband and wife whose lives were devastated by war.

For a soul-searcher in the Information Age who thought it was irrational or anti-intellectual to think he or she has been here before or will be here again, there is rational, perhaps even scientific, ground for believing what tradition taught long ago.

Notes

1. As it is written, "You shall also consider in your heart that as a man chastens his son, so the Lord your God chas-

tened you" (Deuteronomy 8:5).
2. Heard from Rabbi Ezriel Tauber.
3. *Many Lives, Many Masters*, p. 172.
4. *Ma'asiyot MiTzaddikei Yesodei Olam* (Podgorze, 1903), section 5; Moshe Yosef Friedlander, *Batei Avot* (Jerusalem, 1965), pp. 130–31.
5. Nachmanides (Moses ben Nachman, 1194–1270, also known as Ramban), according to some the medieval scholar most representative of normative Judaism, remarks that reincarnation solves all difficulties of why bad things happen to good people (see his discourse on Ecclesiastes and his commentary to Job).
6. *Many Lives, Many Masters*, pp. 172–73.
7. Vilna Gaon, commentary on Jonah.
8. *Many Lives, Many Masters*, p. 120.
9. Noteworthy is the fact that this statement can be found almost verbatim in the following Talmudic maxim: "Do not be like servants who serve the master on condition of reward; rather, be like servants who serve even without the expectation of reward" (*Avot* 1:3).
10. Genesis 2:23.
11. *Sotah* 2a.
12. *Sha'ar HaGilgulim*, ch. 8.
13. Ibid.
14. Ibid.
15. Ibid., ch. 20.

LIFE

A Philosophy of Soul

> Everything can be taken from a man but one thing: the last of the human freedoms — to choose one's attitudes in any given set of circumstances, to choose one's own way.
>
> *Dr. Viktor E. Frankl, author of Man's Search for Meaning*

What is life?[1] That question is so often repeated and so broad, and so many different people have tried to answer it in so many ways, that we are skeptical of anyone who even attempts to address it. Nevertheless, it is a question we must ask if we hope to come to a deeper understanding of what it means to have a soul. After all, even if we believe that each of us is truly a soul rooted in eternity, what are we doing here in this temporal life? What purpose is served by submitting an eternal soul to a life of suffering, mundane responsibilities, and death? Let it stay in eternity and never know the limitations of this world.

What, then, is the purpose of life?

Life is a finite arena where the infinite soul is given the opportunity to earn its eternity. If the individual soul remained in the womb of eternity, its eternity — its most defining attribute — would be nothing more than a gift, a handout, it happened to possess.[2] Through the process of life, though, the soul's panoramic vision becomes clouded. This constriction of awareness results in the opportunity of free choice — finite life affords the infinite soul the possibility to freely choose between infinity and the finite, to declare itself a citizen of heaven, a denizen of eternity, in a truly self-initiating, meaningful way.

Thus, choice — the choice between the infinite and the finite — defines the essence of life. And there is no moment without its choice. Do we help that person in need or do we avert our eyes and pretend we do not see? Do we stand up for our values or do we crumble under pressure from others? Are we easy to forgive or do we allow perceived feelings of personal affront to fester? Are we living up to our responsibilities as a spouse, parent, child, community member?

The choices latent in a given moment need not be restricted only to the interpersonal sphere. The intrapersonal sphere — our ongoing, private inner world — provides the richest harvest of choices. Are we honest with ourselves or are we escaping responsibility? Are we absorbed in noble thoughts or are our minds focused on trivialities? Are we seeking answers or are we looking for excuses?

A Philosophy of Soul

Maimonides, the famous medieval Talmudist and philosopher, wrote that a righteous act performed when no one else is looking is in many ways greater than a righteous act performed in public.[3] People are naturally predisposed to perform acts based on what others will think of them; if they do good things in public, it is usually out of the desire for public recognition. Actions performed in private, on the other hand, are often the barometer of greatness because they are performed exclusively due to the person's own internal conscience.

For instance, how often do we hear people say, "It's illegal only if you get caught." Getting caught may be the criterion for the legal system, but it reveals the fact that the person is completely incognizant (whether willfully or unwillfully) that an inner reality is calling him or her to responsibility. Thus, one can achieve the greatest heights when one has the opportunity, say, to steal money without getting caught but does not do so. It will not make the front page, and no one else in the world might know of it, but it demonstrates that one is dedicated to the laws of the soul. The inner life of a person is therefore a potpourri of choices.

In addition to the interpersonal and intrapersonal spheres, however, there is also the suprapersonal sphere, a person's relationship with his or her Creator — God. Ultimately, all our acts — private and public — must have God in mind; more than anything else, such thoughts can truly be said to affirm the soul's devotion to the Infinite Reality.

This idea may sound alien to some people raised in a secularized society. But what value, really, do the intrapersonal and suprapersonal spheres have in a worldview devoid of an all-knowing Higher Power?

Herein lies the real secret to feeling that every moment and nuance of one's life has meaning. If you know that not only every action, but every thought and motivation, possesses the potential to fulfill life's purpose, you would not trade the moment for anything; you would be grateful for every moment of life. With such an outlook, even suffering or tragedy — no less than any other life situation — give one the opportunity for choice and therefore have meaning. In fact, adversity offers the greatest opportunity for heroic choice.

If we understood the opportunity that is contained within each moment, we would live our lives differently; we would discover an entirely new value to the concept of time. How much is a moment worth? It depends. If you think in terms of the temporal, then the moment is only a matter of seconds. After those few seconds, it will never return. If, on the other hand, you know that every moment possesses the potential to fulfill life's purpose, then you would not trade it for anything; you would fight for every moment of life. You would love life deeply because you would know that it is all a gift, every bit of it — even a life of external restrictions.

Belief in the eternity of the soul is not antithetical to the belief that the value of this finite life is infinitely precious.

A Philosophy of Soul

To the contrary, the two are interdependent. This life is a time of development for the soul, an opportunity for it to be able to eternally feel that it has earned its infinity and not just received it as a handout. If one does not believe in one's eternity, one cannot maximally feel the meaning of each moment. One can perhaps say that a moment of life is priceless without that belief, but one will have a difficult time actualizing it into real-life circumstances.

The Midrash describes the last moments of Moses' life.[4] Surprisingly — almost shockingly — it tells us that he begged and pleaded with God to let him live longer. Moses was 120 years old at the time and who had accomplished more than he had? Yet he begged for life. Was he afraid to die? Did he harbor doubts whether he was eternal? That could not be, for the Bible describes him as the most unique prophet, the only one "whom God knew face to face."[5] Moses not only knew he was eternal but realized that death would provide him an opportunity to experience God infinitely more closely than he could in an earthly existence. Why, then, did he beg God for extra life?

Imagine you were told that you would be allowed into a diamond mine for one hour to pick up all the diamonds you could find. It's hot and stuffy. You are grimy and covered with dirt. Your feet ache, and your back feels like it's breaking, but when that hour is up you beg to have a few extra minutes, because the temporary discomfort is worth the unique opportunity to collect as many diamonds as you can.

That was Moses. He knew that every moment of this life, no matter how inferior to eternal life, was an opportunity to pick up diamonds. And in the eternal life, each of those diamonds would be of infinite value. Thus, no one more than he understood the value of life.

A person who claims that belief in the eternity of the soul perforce makes people reckless toward life does not understand the meaning of life. Genuine belief in one's immortality should never be an excuse for carelessness. Interestingly, renewed appreciation for life is almost invariably the attitude of people who have had near-death experiences. Concurrent with a heightened awareness of the beauty of the afterlife, NDErs gain a sense of the value of the present life.

A moment of life is priceless. Literally. In all the vast expanse of infinite existence there is nothing else like this little island of finite time called life. Therefore, every moment, no matter how intermeshed with suffering, is of infinite value and meaning.

The idea may be difficult for some readers. They may cite, for instance, the Holocaust. How could life in a concentration camp in any way, shape, or form be construed as meaningful? However, just the opposite is true: the Holocaust is the greatest proof that every moment has meaning. At least, this was the experience of a world-renowned Holocaust survivor, a man famous for founding logotherapy, a type of psychotherapy that has been described as the "third school of Viennese psychiatry" (after

A Philosophy of Soul 163

Freud and Adler). His name is Viktor Frankl.

The general details of his experience, covering three years in Nazi concentration camps (including time in the most notorious, Auschwitz), can be found in the first part of his classic book, *Man's Search for Meaning*. Already an accomplished Viennese psychiatrist before the war came to Europe, it can safely be said that nothing taught Viktor Frankl more about human nature than his experience in the camps. "Life in a concentration camp," he wrote, "tore open the human soul and exposed its depths."[6]

The common denominator of all those who experienced the concentration camp was the complete stripping away of their previous sense of identity. Bankers and lawyers were treated no differently than beggars and liars. "We all had once been or had fancied ourselves to be 'somebody.' Now we were treated like complete nonentities," Dr. Frankl wrote.[7] Worse, though, than the loss of societal status was the way camp life could strip one of one's human status.

> Under the influence of a world which no longer recognized the value of human life and human dignity, the personal ego finally suffered a loss of values. If the man in the concentration camp did not struggle against this in a last effort to save his self-respect, he lost the feeling of being an individual, a being with a mind, with inner freedom and personal "value"....[8]

Into this whirlwind of sand-blasted, raw existence and formless, shifting sands of human value, Dr. Frankl, like so many others, found himself. However, he, with his honed skills of introspection and observation, also discovered an incredible insight that gave his entire experience, and indeed his life, profound meaning:

> The experiences of camp life show that man does have a choice of action.... There were always choices to make. Every day, every hour, offered the opportunity to make a decision, a decision which determined whether you would or would not submit to those powers which threatened to rob you of your very self, your inner freedom....[9]

In describing an example of one such decision, Dr. Frankl related the following story concerning himself:

> I remember a personal experience. Almost in tears from pain (I had terrible sores on my feet from wearing torn shoes), I limped a few kilometers with our long column of men from the camp to our work site. Very cold, bitter winds struck us. I kept thinking of the endless little problems of our miserable life. What would there be to eat tonight? If a piece of sausage came as extra ration, should I exchange it for a piece of bread? Should I trade my last cigarette, which was left from a bonus I received a fortnight ago, for a bowl of soup? How could I get a piece of wire to replace the fragment

which served as one of my shoelaces? Would I get to our work site in time to join my usual working party, or would I have to join another, which might have a brutal foreman? What could I do to get on good terms with the *kapo*, who could help me obtain work in camp instead of undertaking this horribly long daily march?

> I became disgusted with the state of affairs which compelled me, daily and hourly, to think of only such trivial things. I forced my thoughts to turn to another subject. Suddenly, I saw myself standing on the platform of a well-lit, warm, and pleasant lecture room. In front of me sat an attentive audience on comfortable upholstered seats. I was giving a lecture on the psychology of the concentration camp! All that oppressed me at that moment became objective, seen and described from the remote viewpoint of science. By this method I succeeded somehow in rising above the situation, above the sufferings of the moment....[10]

Frankl had so raised himself above the situation that he would later tell audiences that the real explanation for why he survived while others gave up was that in the midst of his suffering he took control of his thoughts and envisioned himself lecturing about his experiences. "What kept me alive was you," he has told audiences. "Others gave up hope. I dreamed. I dreamed that someday I would be here, telling you how I, Viktor Frankl, had survived the Nazi concentration camps. I've never seen you before, I've never seen any of you before, I've never given this speech before. But in my dreams, in my dreams, I have stood before you and said these words a thousand times."[11]

Dr. Frankl's recognition of his and others' indomitable inner freedom under the most restrictive and oppressive conditions demonstrated conclusively that "everything can be taken from a man but one thing: the last of the human freedoms — to choose one's attitudes in any given set of circumstances, to choose one's own way."[12]

If a human being in a concentration camp, stripped of every material and moral cover, still has choices — albeit not necessarily external — then there is not one situation in life without its choice. Frankl's lifework, therefore, is testimony that every moment in life is pregnant with purpose — there are no moments devoid of choice — and that life, therefore, even in a concentration camp, is ultimately not meaningless. That is the most important lesson to learn and remember. Life is never devoid of choices and meanings.

Every life situation ultimately boils down to the choice between something of finite value versus something of infinite value, and the soul is placed between these poles in order to give it the opportunity to voluntarily connect itself, in its nethermost depths, to the roots of eternity. The greater number of times it opts for the infinite, the more it deserves the eternity bequeathed it — the more it makes itself a creature of eternity rather than merely existing as a creature bequeathed eternity.

Of course, the criterion is not just quantitative. Every choice possesses a qualitative component as well. A single, deeply felt, understood, and consciously made choice can affect the root of one's existence more so than an entire lifetime of choices. And that is really the reason a single moment is priceless. One moment can uncover an insight or meaning that suddenly swings open a previously hidden doorway that leads an individual to the far end of his personal universe. One moment can define an entire life. And any given moment can be that moment. Therefore, a moment is truly priceless.

Qualitative, defining moments are nowhere more poignantly expressed than in life-and-death situations. In 1929, rioting Arabs in the city of Hebron entered a yeshivah (Jewish boys' school) and started killing indiscriminately. As one teenage boy lay dying in a pool of blood, he noticed that a terrified friend of his had not yet been harmed. Summoning his last ounce of strength, the dying boy called to the friend, "Come here. Lie in my blood. Perhaps they will think you are dead, too."[13]

Such an act in the last moments of one's life is the raw stuff of eternity. That dying boy's last seconds were not mere seconds, but seconds worth a hundred years, seconds that probably most people never equal with an entire lifetime of seconds. The basic meaning of life — choice, inner liberty, inner devotion to one's most essential self — can never be stripped away. If that is true of the Holocaust, then it is true in our daily lives.

"Everyone," Dr. Frankl wrote, "has his own specific vocation or mission in life to carry out a concrete assignment which demands fulfillment. Therein he cannot be replaced, nor can his life be repeated. Thus, everyone's task is as unique as is his specific opportunity to implement it."[14]

The businessperson and the scholar, the career woman and the housewife, the childless couple and the parents with more children than they can handle, the wealthy and the poor, the healthy and the sick, the young and the old — no one is ever at any time withheld from completing the purpose he or she was put in this world. No one.[15]

Why, then, is our world plagued with people who feel that life is meaningless, who are haunted by the experience of an inescapable inner void? Because we do not teach the value of a moment. We do not teach it because we do not believe in it. And we do not believe in it because we do not live it. The present exists, but at the moment we are probably somewhere far, far away. We recycle the past over and over again or generate imaginary scenarios about the good things awaiting us in the future. In either case, the present is far away. A person can live eighty years and yet hardly have lived a year.

People suffering from depression often feel they have no present. They either dwell excessively on the past or fantasize excessively about the future. Living in the past or in the future produces a spiritual and emotional numbness to the present.

Life has pain, and we all have to deal with it. If you do

not feel the pain, you will not feel the pleasure either. A depressed person often fails to realize that pain is not the opposite of pleasure. Numbness, insensitivity, the inability to feel — that is the opposite of pleasure. However, because they believe that pain is the opposite of pleasure, they avoid it at all costs, despite the fact that the thing they should really be avoiding is the numbness. Without the pain, there is no pleasure.

Many of life's real difficulties are beyond our control. But we have the freedom to choose how we react to them. We can neutralize our pain in many ways, but that is not necessarily the best thing to do. It is normal to seek to alleviate our pain and correct it at its source. However, while we experience it, we must not be afraid to confront it head on. Life's difficulties are hidden messages meant to teach us a lesson we may not have yet learned. Those who do learn the lesson come to realize that their suffering harbored redemption, their failure success, their darkness light.

The wonderful thing about writing on a computer with a word processor is that you do not have to fear mistakes. Before computers, if you made a mistake you had to use correction fluid, perhaps even retype the entire paper. Today you simply go back to the point of the mistake and correct it, and the word processor reorganizes the entire page for you.

The same is true of our spiritual mistakes. The past is never completely lost as long as we are alive. In a single, emotionally packed, deeply felt moment, anyone can return to his original status as a citizen of the soul. And when we do, we can correct all our past failings. Like entering a correction into a document on the computer, one moment of return can send ripples of change through all the other moments of our life already passed.

It may not be easy. Nevertheless, such a change can happen in a moment. The real you is the soul-you that hungers for truth. People get depressed because they fail to identify themselves with their soul. To "return" means to become once again the real you — the soul-you that can tolerate only so much lethargy and self-deception. When you failed in the past, that was not you. The real you is the "you" you discover in a moment of naked truth. Such a moment is almost certain to be painful, yet when you uncover — or, rather, rediscover — your real self, you find a part of yourself you can love eternal, and there is no greater pleasure than that.

Spirituality is not about fortune-telling or communicating with spirits. Spirituality is about living the moment. A true sourcebook of spirituality tells us how to live now — this moment we are all part of.

Notes

1. I am indebted to Rabbi Ezriel Tauber for the inspiration and much of the contents of this section.
2. Rabbi Aryeh Kaplan discusses this in his essay "A World of Love," which can be found in *If You Were God* (p. 56). He

A Philosophy of Soul

writes: "Our Sages teach us, 'One who eats another's bread is ashamed to look in his face' (*Yerushalmi, Orlah* 1:3).... Our Sages repeat this lesson any number of times. They teach us that 'when a man must depend on gifts, his face changes.' In another place, they say, 'When one depends on the gifts of others, the world appears dark to him.' Elsewhere they proclaim, 'One who eats at another's table is never satisfied' (*Berachot* 6b; *Beitzah* 32b; *Avot D'Rabbi Natan* 31:1). God wanted the good that He would give to be perfect good, not tinged by any shame. If it were given as a free gift, however, it would always be accompanied by the shame that results from accepting a free gift. The only way to avoid this would be for the good to be earned, so that it would no longer be a gift. It is for this reason that the good that God gives us is only bestowed as a reward for our own actions. When the *Zohar* speaks of the ultimate world of good, it says, 'Happy is he who comes here without shame.' This is actually echoing the words of the prophet, who said, 'And you shall eat and be satisfied...and my people shall never be ashamed' (Jeremiah 2:26)."

3. He cites the case of biblical Josef resisting the temptation of his master's wife as the paradigm of such righteousness.
4. *Devarim Rabbah* 11:6.
5. Deuteronomy 34:10.
6. *Man's Search for Meaning*, p. 94.
7. Ibid., p. 72.
8. Ibid., p. 60.
9. Ibid., pp. 74–75.
10. Ibid., pp. 81–82.

11. In *Swim with the Sharks without Being Eaten Alive*, by Harvey Mackey, p. 73.
12. *Man's Search for Meaning*, p. 75.
13. This story was printed in *The Fire Within*, by Rabbi Hillel Goldberg (Mesorah Publications, 1987), p. 167.
14. *Man's Search for Meaning*, p. 113.
15. "Each person is created to achieve a specific purpose that is exclusive to him alone. Each moment of life is designated for the fulfillment of a specific task that is also exclusive to that moment. It cannot be achieved at any other time. This is the meaning of the *mishnah* ['If I am not for myself who will be?' — *Avot* 1:14]: If I do not achieve the exclusive purpose for which I was created, no one can accomplish it. If I do not fulfill the specific task that was designated for this time, it can never again be attained" (*Chiddushei HaRim*, cited in *Metzudah Pirkei Avot*, by Rabbi Avraham Davis [Metzudah Publications, 1980], p. 31).

Appendixes

Appendix A
Afterlife in Scripture

Many people today, including Jews and non-Jews, are surprised to find out that Judaism has always espoused belief in the existence of an afterlife and that there are references to it in the written text. The Torah consistently promises this-worldly reward for performance of its commandments: a fruitful land, children, peace, prosperity. Things people can see with their eyes. Nevertheless, just because the Torah emphasizes this-worldly reward (and, conversely, this-worldly punishment) doesn't mean it does not support belief in other-worldly reward and punishment. The Oral Torah (the Talmud, Midrash, *Zohar*) is full of details about the afterlife. However, even the Written Torah is filled with references to it.

The place to begin is in the Garden of Eden.[1] Adam

and Eve are told not to eat from the Tree of Knowledge of Good and Evil. They disobey. God says:

> The human being has become like one of us, knowing good and evil. If he stretches forth his hand and takes from the Tree of Life and eats, he will live forever.[2]

Consequently, God expels Adam and Eve from the Garden of Eden and places sword-bearing angelic beings to "guard the way to the Tree of Life."[3] We see from this that the Bible is cognizant of the possibility of human immortality. If human beings could somehow eat from the Tree of Life, they would "live forever." We see also that the Tree of Life still exists. Though guarded by angels, the Tree of Life survives Adam and Eve's expulsion.

The implication is that if somehow the angels were removed and the tree left unguarded, as it originally was, immortality could be attained by human beings. There is certainly nothing to suggest that the angels' station there is intended to be permanent. It is even possible to say that though the angels are on guard they might allow certain worthy individuals access to the Tree of Life. Whatever the case, the fact that the Garden of Eden episode talks openly about such a tree, that it was not destroyed, and that its location is named, if not known, indicates at the very least that the Bible contains the doctrine of immortality and even suggests the tantalizing possibility of humans attaining it.

Furthermore, note that the entire issue of humans partaking of the Tree of Life and living forever is said in reference to the possibility of bodily immortality. It is not merely the soul but the body that will live forever should Adam eat from the tree. Concerning the soul (or spiritual element), Adam is said to have blown into him by God a "soul of life."[4] Even if, as some say, the correct translation here is that God blew into Adam the "breath of life," the impression is that he received something emanating from inside the Eternal God.

The word *life* here is particularly significant because, as is evident from the reference to the Tree of Life, the Hebrew word for life means eternal life. The implication, therefore, is that God blew into Adam a "soul" or "breath" of eternal life.

The Scripture tells us that the first human was created with two opposing forces — the material and the spiritual:

> Then God formed the human from the dust of the ground [i.e., material] and breathed into his nostrils the breath [or soul] of life; and the human became a living being.[5]

Note that instead of the verse saying, "And God *placed* into the human a living soul," it says that He *blew* into him a living soul. The image implies a transference of sorts; just as one who blows air transfers air from within himself into the one to whom he is blowing into, so too God transferred something from within Himself into man. The verse is thus not merely stating that God gave us the ability to breathe and be alive in a physical sense, but also that God gave us a part of Himself, an actual spiritual quality — a soul.

The original sin may lead to the tragic reality of physical death, but not necessarily to spiritual death — death of the soul-spiritual element. As can be deduced from this and other biblical references, connection to an element of eternity (be it soul, breath, life, or whatever) is part of man's natural predisposition.[6] The body may go down to the pit, but "the spirit returns to the God Who gave it."[7]

Let's briefly mention a few other verses that demonstrate that the doctrine of immortality is endemic to the Written Torah.

The death of Abraham, Isaac, Jacob, Ishmael, Aaron, and Moses are described with the conspicuous phrase "and he was gathered to his people."[8] In each of these circumstances the phrase pertains to the afterlife. For instance, concerning Abraham the sequence goes:

> Then he [Abraham] expired. And Abraham died in good old age and full of years. And he was gathered to his people. And his sons Isaac and Ishmael buried him in the Cave of Machpeileh....[9]

Abraham was the first of the patriarchs to be buried in the Cave of Machpeilah. Who, then, was he gathered to? Obviously the phrase "gathered to his people" cannot be talking about the physical cemetery. Since immediately before this it says that he had already died, this phrase certainly refers to the afterlife.

Similarly, Aaron and Moses were buried alone, and still it says that each was "gathered to his people." All these verses indicate that after death the souls of these people joined the souls of their fathers and other righteous ancestors in the afterlife.

The existence of an afterlife was so self-understood in Scripture that it even prohibits contacting the spirit of the dead.[10] If the Torah didn't believe in an afterlife, why would it prohibit contact with dead spirits?

Moving from the Five Books to the Prophets we find in Samuel[11] that the spirit of Samuel the prophet was conjured up to speak to King Saul. Samuel, as a spirit, tells the despondent king that because of his sin "you and your sons [who were about to go with him to battle the Philistines] will be with me tomorrow." This verse clearly states that Saul and his sons will perish the next day in battle, which they did, and then join Samuel in the afterlife.

In the second book of Samuel,[12] King David loses a newborn child. After much fasting and praying to no avail David returns to normal life stating, "Can I cause him to return anymore? I am going to him; he's not returning to me." David was consoling himself that at least eventually he would meet his son in the World to Come.

In Writings, we have a direct reference:

> Everything is going to one place. We all come from the earth, and we all return to the earth. [However] who knows [and understands the] spirit of man-

> kind, which goes up [to the heavens] as opposed to the spirit of an animal, which goes down below into the earth.[13]

Similarly,

> The dust will return to the ground as it was [in its original state] and the spirit will return to God Who gave it.[14]

We see clearly that the spirit does not die with the death of the body. It returns to Heaven and to God.

And so, even from this limited sample of verses we see clearly that the Written Torah definitely promotes the idea over and over again in many different ways.

Of course, a natural question rises that if the doctrine is so ingrained in the biblical outlook, why is it not stated more descriptively or systematically?

First, one does not elaborate upon that which is obvious. The *New York Times* does not quote the Constitution in every article about an accused criminal put on trial. In the ancient world, an afterlife in one form or another was taken for granted. If anything, the phenomenon that the afterlife, wherever it is implied, is expressed matter-of-factly provides additional evidence in favor of the doctrine.

Another possible reason the afterlife is mentioned in only a general way and relatively infrequently in Scripture is because the entire thrust of the Torah is the celebration and responsibility of living life — this life. It does not want to invoke (and risk abusing) the argument of reward or punishment in some afterlife. One should strive for the moral and spiritual ideals promoted in the Torah for their own sake. This should not be taken to mean that the Torah denies the possibility of otherworldly reward, but rather that it wants to highlight the importance of intrinsic motivations when pursuing eternal values.[15]

The bottom line is that the contention that the Written Torah does not mention the afterlife at all is simply not true. To the contrary, belief in an afterlife in the Written Torah is so deeply embedded that it is taken for granted, and that is why statements about it appear matter-of-factly.

Notes

1. From a philosophical point of view (as opposed to an exclusively textual point of view), the place to begin is "In the beginning..." (Genesis 1:1). The mere statement that an All-Powerful, benevolent Creator created the universe leads to the conclusion that the pinnacle of that creation, the human being, is destined to receive the reward of immortality. At the very least, it would be against all logic to conclude that such a Creator had this world of injustice, deprivation, pain, and ultimately death as the final arena of His original design. Philosophically speaking, therefore, the idea of an afterlife is a natural extension of the premise of one God.
2. Genesis 3:22.
3. Ibid., 24.
4. Ibid. 2:7.
5. Ibid.

6. This is substantiated by the statement, mentioned several times throughout the Five Books of Moses, that certain sins result in a life or soul getting "cut off"(Leviticus 22:3, 23:29–30; Numbers 15:31). By implication, if such sins are not committed, the soul remains "connected" to the source of eternal life. Connection is the soul's natural state. This is the stance of the classic biblical commentator Nachmanides (in his commentary to Leviticus 18:9).
7. Ecclesiastes 12:7.
8. Genesis 25:8; ibid. 35:29; ibid. 49:33; ibid. 25:17; Numbers 20:24; and Numbers 27:13 and Deuteronomy 32:50 respectively.
9. Genesis 25:8–9.
10. Leviticus 19:31, 20:6, 20:27; Deuteronomy 18:10–12.
11. I Samuel 28:19.
12. II Samuel 12:23.
13. Ecclesiastes 3:20–21.
14. Ibid. 12:7.
15. See *Chovot HaLevavot*, *Sha'ar HaBitachon*, section 4; *Kli Yakar*, Leviticus 26:12.

Appendix B
Hints of Soul

In addition to all the verses that tell us of the soul's existence, it's possible to identify the existence of the soul in humans by contemplating different human feelings, attitudes, emotions, and behavior — in a word, through our own experience.

For instance, we see that when we do an extraordinarily good deed we feel very good about it. After a person has finished an intense prayer or after he has overcome a desire to do wrong — even if he just held himself back from saying a slightly derogatory statement about someone else — he feels very good deep inside. The question is, why? Why should a body made of flesh and bone feel good about a nonphysical accomplishment?

Moreover, even someone who is not particularly sensitive to his spiritual side can experience these feelings. What else but something like the existence of a soul can explain the good feelings felt in even the most spiritually insensitive people?

Looking at the other side of the coin, how does a person who did a bad deed feel guilt? What is guilt? Where do such feelings come from? Someone might answer that it comes from the human conscience. But what is the conscience? Where does it come from? And if one wants to say we feel guilty because society beat into us a sense of right and wrong, then we ask him, who started society? Was it not people who were told by earlier people, who were told by earlier people, and so on, what is right and wrong? And where did those original people get their conscience from?

The logical answer is a soul, something otherworldly within us that itself is naturally endowed with divine qualities.

There are other ways to perceive the existence of the soul. For instance, how can we explain that powerful longing and sublime feelings experienced when listening to beautiful music or when observing the sun setting or viewing a majestic mountain range in the distance? Or sometimes all of a sudden we are aroused by our life situation and ask, "What am I doing with my life?" or "What is going to happen to me?" or "When will I change?" What arouses that need for introspection and spiritual longing? What else, really, could it be but something like a soul?

Yet another way to come to a rational understanding that human beings possess a soul is when we hear stories about depraved, corrupt, and even vicious criminals who all of a sudden experience a moment of regret. It makes sense to say that this might emanate from something like the soul, a preexisting quality bequeathed to every person. As much as the hardened criminal's good nature had been covered up, it can always, at any moment, burst to the surface unexpectedly. And if it was more than a one-time moment of regret or good deed — if the person actually turned over a new leaf and started living a consistently moral life — what else can really account for the turnaround?

Perhaps the person is not a criminal but simply an individual immersed in a materialistic lifestyle. Suddenly he follows through on a yearning to become spiritual. What gives this person the strength to sacrifice his physical pleasures for a higher ideal or principle if not the soul, which intuitively knows the value of the spiritual endeavors? How else would there be people willing to forfeit their comforts and sometimes even their lives for what they perceive as a higher good? What force can convince a person to forfeit his whole physical being, if not the Godly soul?

Another window to the existence of the soul is the inborn feeling of embarrassment we humans possess. If we are nothing more than intelligent animals, why should we be embarrassed to stand naked or to be seen performing any of our bodily functions? To think that these feelings exist only because we were trained this way is a weak argument. The question is, why does society train their offspring in this way? Why did the first societies try to cover up?

The answer is that it's another hint that we have a soul.

Another avenue of evidence for the existence of the soul can be discerned when we analyze the human condition. We find that there are numerous drives that only humans possess that indicate that man is more than just his animalistic tendencies. For instance, we find in human beings an insatiable desire for amassing possessions and money. At the same time, people also crave happiness. Furthermore, only human beings have such an overwhelming need for glory (and not merely as a means to attaining money and/or happiness, but glory for its own sake). Or consider, simply, the desire to accomplish. We are not satisfied merely with our physical preservation; we want to feel we did something useful. Where do these drives come from if not from a soul?

What about the need for self-perpetuation? Where does it come from? It's a universal human longing to want a child. The average person wants to leave something behind when he leaves the world. Even childless couples will often seek to adopt a child even though it will mean undergoing the hardships of raising a child and all the expenses that go along with it.

It's all for the purpose of self-perpetuation. If you leave a child behind, you feel you're still somewhat alive. And if a person is about to leave this world without children, he will often arrange that his money be used for some good cause or to dedicate a building and have his name put on it. Even the wealthy miser, who is so selfish that he will set a large portion of his will to the self-perpetuation of his name rather than to his family, expresses this irrational need for remembrance after death by erecting a mausoleum or an extravagant monument.

The question is, why? What is this drive for posthumous glory?

The answer is that spiritual, eternal entities want to accomplish spiritual, eternal accomplishments. Since the soul intuitively knows that besides its coming from an eternal source it will also return to its eternal source, it instinctively wants to accomplish something that will endure. The human need for perpetuation, then, is an expression of the soul.

It's also interesting to note that people have a strong desire to live long, as well as an instinctive fear of death. Of course, younger and even older people who are healthy will obviously want to continue to live long. But how do we understand that sick or very old people desire to keep living?

Again, these feelings can be said to emanate from the soul, because it knows the tremendous value of every second of life as well as the foreknowledge of the accounting it will undergo regarding the time spent in its bodily form. These are not feelings of the body, but of the soul.

Finally, if you attend almost any funeral where a eulogy is delivered, chances are the speaker will attempt to find some spiritually redeeming quality in the deceased — even if the deceased was not a very good person! When delivering a eulogy, one doesn't say, "This person was so great. He owned a Rolls Royce, a yacht, a private plane, and three summer homes." People realize that once a person is lying there in the ground all his material accomplishments cease to matter. What really counts are the spiritual accomplishments. So, again, we have a universal phenomenon that indicates that all people deep down realize that what really matters is the spirit.

Why would that be if not for the voice of the human soul?

> *The material for this chapter originated from a series of lectures by Rabbi Shmuel Waldman, the contents of which eventually became the book Beyond a Reasonable Doubt (Feldheim Publishers, 2002).*

Bibliography

Dossey, Larry, M.D. *Healing Words: The Power of Prayer and the Practice of Medicine.* Harper Mass Market Paperbacks, 1997.

———. *Reinventing Medicine.* New York: HarperCollins, 1999.

Edwards, Paul. *Reincarnation: A Critical Examination.* Prometheus Books, 1996.

Frankl, Viktor. *Man's Search for Meaning.* Washington Square Press, 1997.

Goldberg, Rabbi Chaim Binyamin. *Mourning in Halacha: The Laws and Customs of the Year of Mourning.* New York: Mesorah Publications, 1991.

Jung, Carl Gustav. *Modern Man in Search of a Soul.* Harvest Books, 1955.

Kaplan, Rabbi Aryeh. *If You Were God: Three Works by Aryeh Kaplan.* OU/NCSY, 1983.

———. *The Handbook of Jewish Thought.* Vol. 2. Moznaim, 1992.

Kubler-Ross, Elizabeth. *On Death and Dying.* New York: Macmillan Publishing, 1969.

Mackey, Harvey. *Swim with the Sharks without Being Eaten Alive.* New York: Ivy Books, 1988.

Moody, Raymond, M.D. *Life After Life: The Investigation of a Phenomenon — Survival of Bodily Death.* Harper San Francisco, 1975.

Moody, Raymond, M.D., and Paul Perry. *Coming Back: A Psychiatrist Explores Past-Life Journeys.* Bantam, 1991.

———. *The Light Beyond.* Bantam, 1988.

Morse, Melvin, M.D. *Closer to the Light: Learning from Near-Death Experiences of Children.* New York: Ivy Books, 1991.

Morse, Melvin, M.D., and Paul Perry. *Transformed by the Light: The Powerful Effect of Near-Death Experiences on People's Lives.* Villard Books, 1992.

Ring, Kenneth. *Heading Toward Omega: In Search of the Meaning of the Near-Death Experience.* William Morrow & Company, 1984.

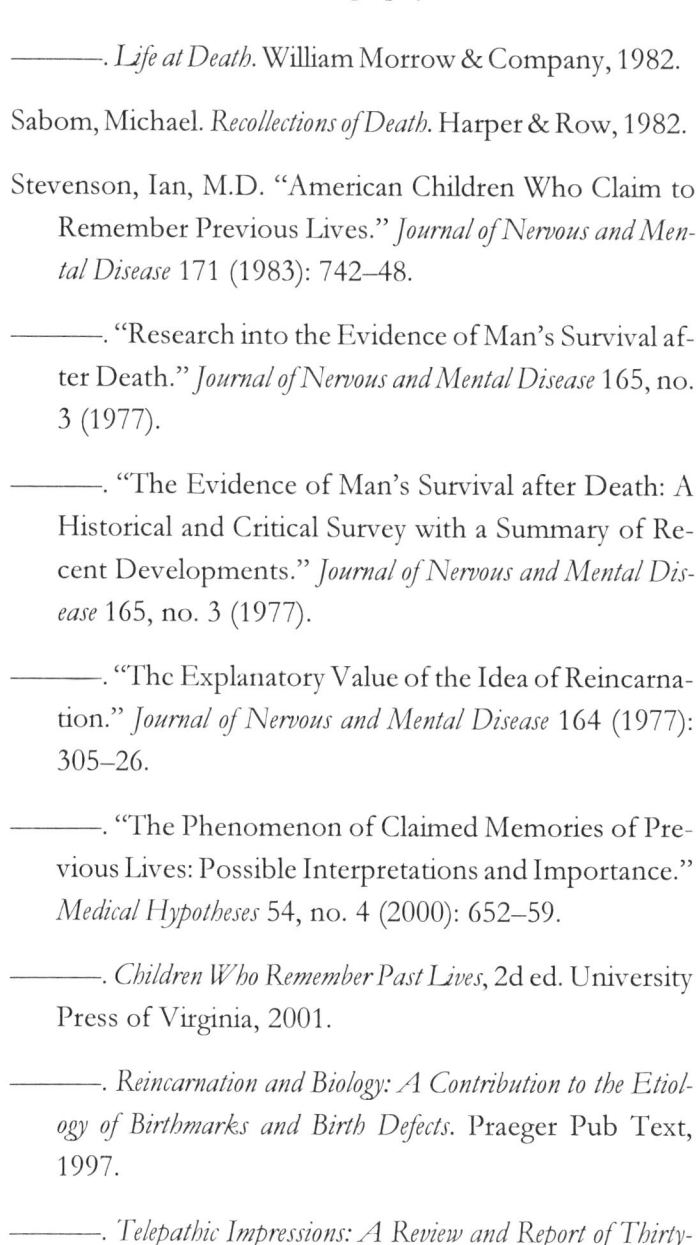

———. *Life at Death*. William Morrow & Company, 1982.

Sabom, Michael. *Recollections of Death*. Harper & Row, 1982.

Stevenson, Ian, M.D. "American Children Who Claim to Remember Previous Lives." *Journal of Nervous and Mental Disease* 171 (1983): 742–48.

———. "Research into the Evidence of Man's Survival after Death." *Journal of Nervous and Mental Disease* 165, no. 3 (1977).

———. "The Evidence of Man's Survival after Death: A Historical and Critical Survey with a Summary of Recent Developments." *Journal of Nervous and Mental Disease* 165, no. 3 (1977).

———. "The Explanatory Value of the Idea of Reincarnation." *Journal of Nervous and Mental Disease* 164 (1977): 305–26.

———. "The Phenomenon of Claimed Memories of Previous Lives: Possible Interpretations and Importance." *Medical Hypotheses* 54, no. 4 (2000): 652–59.

———. *Children Who Remember Past Lives*, 2d ed. University Press of Virginia, 2001.

———. *Reincarnation and Biology: A Contribution to the Etiology of Birthmarks and Birth Defects*. Praeger Pub Text, 1997.

———. *Telepathic Impressions: A Review and Report of Thirty-*

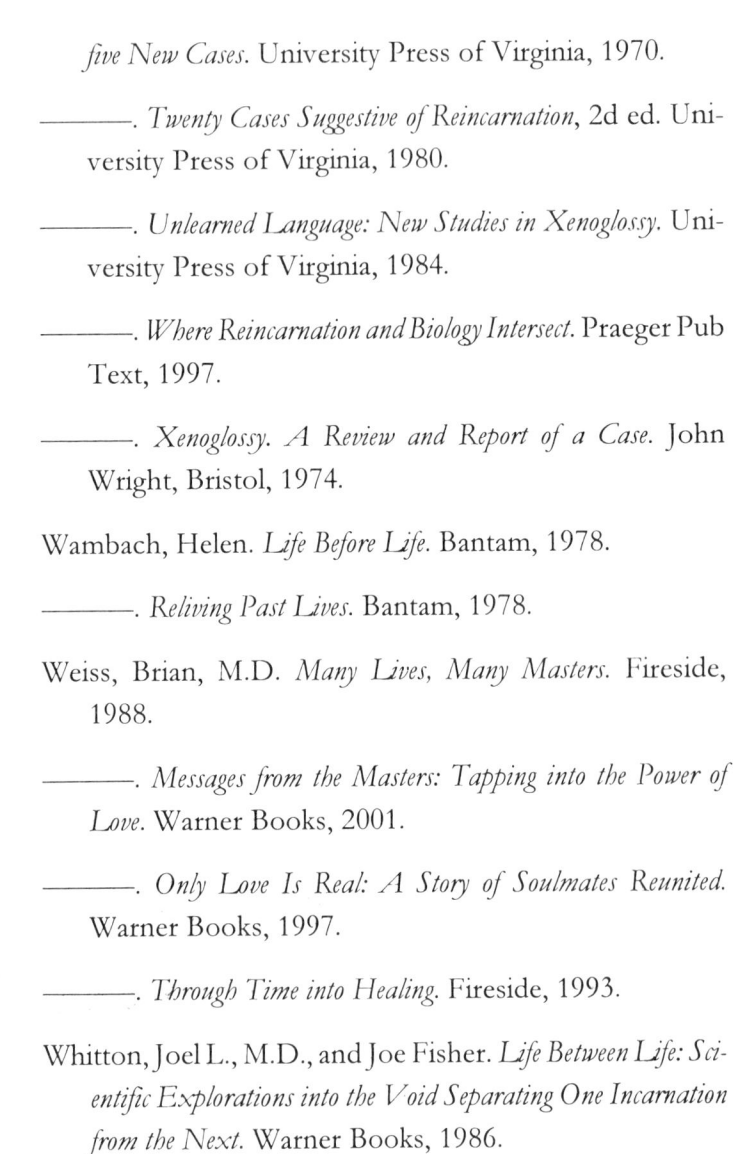

five New Cases. University Press of Virginia, 1970.

———. *Twenty Cases Suggestive of Reincarnation*, 2d ed. University Press of Virginia, 1980.

———. *Unlearned Language: New Studies in Xenoglossy*. University Press of Virginia, 1984.

———. *Where Reincarnation and Biology Intersect*. Praeger Pub Text, 1997.

———. *Xenoglossy. A Review and Report of a Case*. John Wright, Bristol, 1974.

Wambach, Helen. *Life Before Life*. Bantam, 1978.

———. *Reliving Past Lives*. Bantam, 1978.

Weiss, Brian, M.D. *Many Lives, Many Masters*. Fireside, 1988.

———. *Messages from the Masters: Tapping into the Power of Love*. Warner Books, 2001.

———. *Only Love Is Real: A Story of Soulmates Reunited*. Warner Books, 1997.

———. *Through Time into Healing*. Fireside, 1993.

Whitton, Joel L., M.D., and Joe Fisher. *Life Between Life: Scientific Explorations into the Void Separating One Incarnation from the Next*. Warner Books, 1986.

About the Author

The author is a former yeshivah teacher and principal with a master's degree in special education. He has written and edited more than twenty books, including *Sefer Nehemiah* and volume 1 of *Trei Asar* in the ArtScroll Tanach series and all eleven of Rabbi Ezriel Tauber's books. He has also published numerous articles in *The Jewish Observer* and other publications, written scripts for the radio program *Taste of Torah*, and taught in various outreach capacities. He lives in Spring Valley, New York, with his family.